P9-CDJ-786

INTERNATIONAL CONNOISSEUR'S
GUIDE TO CIGARS

INTERNATIONAL CONNOISSEUR'S

GUIDE TO
CIGARS

The Art of Selecting and Smoking

Jane Resnick

**Photographs by
George W. Wieser**

BLACK DOG
& LEVENTHAL
PUBLISHERS
NEW YORK

Copyright © 1996 Black Dog & Leventhal Publishers, Inc.

All rights reserved. No part of this book may be reproduced in any form or
by any electronic or mechanical means including information storage and retrieval
systems without written permission of the publisher.

Published by

Black Dog & Leventhal Publishers, Inc.
151 West 19th Street
New York, NY 10011

Distributed by

Workman Publishing Company
708 Broadway
New York, NY 10003
Printed and bound in the U.S.A.

ISBN: 1-884822-88-6

p o n m l

ACKNOWLEDGEMENTS

Many thanks to the following people whose help was invaluable:

Laurence Sherman who permitted us to photograph
in his extraordinary store, Nat Sherman, 500 Fifth Avenue,
New York, NY 10110 (212) 246-5500.

Margery Dine who so graciously accomodated us
at Nat Sherman and provided us with cigars.

Liz Facchiano at J•R Tobacco of America for helping us
prop the photo shoot with cigars. 1-800-J•R-CIGAR.

Mike Butera of Butera Pipe Company.

De La Concha Tobacconist, New York and its staff:
Gomez, Jeff, Robert, Frank, Rob, and Abel
for all of their assistance.

Home of Tobacco Products, Ligny Valdez, Carlos Londono,
and Raphael Lopez, for letting us photograph cigar rolling.
133 Eighth Ave., New York, NY 10011

Granville Restaurant and Lounge,
40 East 20th St., New York, NY 10003.

Helen Kensinger and Niki Singer at *Cigar Aficionado*.

Fred Horn for his knowledge and assistance.

Nancy Faulker for her assistance at the photo shoots.

Book design by Jonette Jakobson

TABLE OF CONTENTS

INTRODUCTION

The cigar...is something that commands respect.
It is made for all the senses, for all the pleasures,
for the nose, the palate, the fingers, the eyes...
A good cigar contains the promise of
a totally pleasurable experience.

Zino Davidoff
author, **The Connoisseur's Book of the Cigar**

The ancient Mayans smoked cigars for religious pur-
poses. Today's ardent smokers hold the cigars them-
selves in reverence. Cigars are once again gaining the
respect and appreciation that is their due. In America, at
the end of the twentieth century, we are coming full circle to the closing of the last century, when cigars were a
stylish accessory to prosperous lives. In 1994 cigar sales
in the United States increased for the first time since
1970 when eight billion cigars were sold. In the last year,
sales of premium cigars have risen over 30% and the
current demand for imported cigars is estimated at over
150 million. The members of the worldwide cigar frater-
nity are legion. Ever since a crewman aboard Columbus'
journey to the New World spotted a tobacco smoking
native, men of all societies have been enamored with the
cigar. And now women have joined these masses.

This is no wonder. The enjoyment of a good cigar is
personal and idiosyncratic, yet it can be shared with social
acquaintances and intimate partners. The nuances of cigars are infinite and the possibilities for new experiences
are endless. At the same time, taking pleasure in a famil-
iar cigar is the most satisfying assurance of comfort and
relaxation. Cigars are an enhancement to any lifestyle.

This book strives to be an excellent reference of available cigars. It is a representative listing of the major
brands of premium and mass market cigars. The book
hopes to educate casual smokers, beginners and connoisseurs alike, for the subject can be entered on many levels
and there is always more to learn. And that is the beauty
of smoking cigars. They entice you into new sensations,
and offer wonderful moments of contentment, fleeting
like the smoke of a cigar, but unforgettable.

HOW TOBACCO BECOMES A CIGAR:
From Seed to Smoke

Earth ne'er did breed
Such a jovial weed.

Barten Holyday, 1618

Life's finest moments are ephemeral, even though they may require years of preparation. So it is with cigars. The keen pleasure of an hour spent with a truly gratifying cigar is the result of months, even years, of attentive, specialized, labor-intensive work.

The original all-natural product, cigars begin with a tobacco plant, but not just any sprout growing wild on a tropical hillside. Very few places in the world are blessed with the soil, temperature, and humidity that can nourish a seedling into a plant whose leaves thrive through the cigar-making process. Perfect weather alone is not enough, for the alchemy is in the soil and no two locations are exactly alike. Thus, even in Cuba, the wrapper, binder, and filler tobaccos of home grown *puros* are only cultivated in a few locations, the most famous being the Vuelta Abajo valley in the western part of the country. The finest wrapper in the world, Connecticut's shade-grown leaf, is only planted on one hundred very specific acres in that state. Connecticut wrapper grown in Ecuador may be superb, but it will be different. So no matter how excellent, cigars produced in the Dominican Republic, Honduras, Nicaragua, Mexico, or Cuba cannot be the same. All have idiosyncratic qualities that emanate from their native soils— the irreplaceable underground ingredient.

The life of a premium cigar begins as the tiniest of seeds, hovered over for 45 days in a nursery then planted like so many soldiers in the straightest of rows. Shade-grown tobacco is covered by a tall, tent like structure of cheesecloth or mesh. Another forty-five days, and the plants are ready for their first "priming," the removal of some leaves destined for cigars. The secrets of cigar taste begin to unfold even at this point, for the position of leaves on the stalk gives them different flavors. *Valdo,* the leaf at the bottom has the mildest taste; *seco,* at the midsection, a medium flavor, and *ligero* at the top has the strongest flavor and texture. Even after five or six primings, a tobacco plant only yields sixteen to eighteen leaves that meet the high standards of premium cigar making.

These well-chosen leaves are bundled according to texture and size, and hung in curing barns for anywhere from three to eight weeks, depending on the weather and the desired result. Entering the barns green, the leaves begin to lose their color and turn shades of brown. After their tenure in the barns, they will again be graded and separated, grouped by size, texture, and color, a situation that occurs constantly throughout the preparation process. At this point, they are stacked into twenty-leaf bundles, called "hands," and are ready to begin the all-important fermentation process, the time during which the leaves are transformed from mere vegetation to a treasure store of smoking possibilities.

The hands are piled into freestanding monoliths anywhere from three to six feet high and weighing up to ten thousand pounds. The tight packing of these "bulks" or *burros* effectively shuts out air and sets the stage for fermentation or "sweating" as the process is indelicately known. Slowly, the temperature of the inner leaves begins to rise. Moisture, sap, nicotine, and ammonia are released from the leaves, all of which must be exactly the same grade and temperature so that the process remains uniform. Heat and aroma fill the area as the leaves acquire depth and flavor and character. Monitoring the temperature is a crucial step. Long thermometers are thrust into the bulks as the degrees rise. One hundred and sixty degrees Fahrenheit tips the scales, but the usual temperatures are around 120 degrees—except for the maduro which needs higher temperatures to deepen its color.

When the temperature reaches the desired point, each bulk is "turned," that is, the top hand is removed, shaken out, and placed on the ground to become the bottom of a new bulk. This rebuilding from the bottom up can occur as many as ten times over a period of one to three months, under the scrutiny of those who test for age, texture, and color. Leaves that will become maduro may take as long as six months to reach their rich, intense shades of black and brown. The process is complete when the temperature levels off after turning, but the timetable is a subjective one. *Underfer-*

Cigars in the cigar press

mentation produces a cigar that refuses to stay lit and, worse, tastes harsh or bitter and causes a burning sensation in your chest. But if *overfermentation* occurs, the leaves will be "spent" and tasteless, so without proper fermentation timing, there really is no cigar. When fermentation is complete, the tobacco is again meticulously sorted, labeled according to origin and date, and brought to warehouses for aging, a rest period that may last from one to three years or longer.

When the tobacco emerges from the warehouse it is as brittle as yellowed paper that has been too long in the attic. To become pliable again, the leaves are gently sprayed with water, a procedure called "casing" that involves applying the precise amount of moisture necessary to bring the thirsty leaves back to life. Then, they are ready for the stemming operation, the removal of the stem and, in some cases, the separation of wrapper leaf into the left and right sides in order to assure the proper pattern on a handmade cigar. Finally they are once again examined and separated into filler, binder, and wrapper leaf. It seems almost superfluous to mention, but still worthy to note the amount of detailed hand work that has gone into this process so far—and the leaves are not yet being built into cigars.

Not until the "blender" performs his or her sorcery. The expertise of the blender is an intimate knowledge of every tobacco, how it will taste, the rate at which it will burn, and how it will combine with others. To know the attributes of one tobacco or another is a matter of experience, but to know the flavor and character of their combination is an art. The possibilities are as endless as any artist faces with a blank canvas. So the blender dips into his experience as the painter delves into his imagination and selects the tobacco in exactly the proportions that will give his brand its distinctive taste. His choices are not for publication, for a great deal of what distinguishes one company's cigar from another lies in the blender's hands. After his work is complete, after all the planting, growing, priming, categorizing, fermenting, and aging, the tobacco is, at last, ready to become a real cigar.

THE MAKING OF CIGARS:
Hands On...Or Off

Sublime tobacco! Which from East to West
Cheers the tar's labor or the Turkman's rest.
                                              Lord Byron

Myths are so appealing, and none more than the legend that the best Cuban cigars are rolled between the thighs of virgins. Would that it were that easy. Hands, not thighs, are what it takes to build a fine cigar—numerous skillful, indefatigable pairs of hands.

To understand the marvelous craft of making a cigar, you must first know the attendant vocabulary. Of

The roller in these photographs is Raphael Lopez from The Home of Tobacco Products in New York City. They produce their own custom handmade cigars called Almirante. In the above photos he is placing the cigars in the cigar press.

the two ends of the cigar, the one you smoke is called the "head," and the one you light, the "foot" or "tuck." Wrapped over the head is a small piece of tobacco, the "cap," which slopes down just to the "shoulder" of the cigar. The construction of the cigar has three main components—the filler, binder, and wrapper, and it is

the makeup of these and the way they are assembled that makes all the difference.

The **filler** is the core of the cigar, the essential center, which the binder and then the wrapper will embrace. It is made up of long-leaf filler tobacco leaves that run the entire length of a cigar, or short-leaf filler, smaller cut pieces that are primarily for machine-made cigars. Premium cigars only use long-leaf filler, which assures the same taste along the cigar's length and produces a long ash. At least two or three different tobaccos are generally combined in a quality filler to create a palette of flavors in a cigar.

The **binder** is the first layer of covering for the filler. In a quality cigar, it is a specialized leaf that has the tensile strength to hold the bunch together. Mass-market cigars may use a "homogenized" binder, made up of tobacco parts that have been chopped up and put back together again. The binder affects the taste, burn rate, and aroma of a cigar, and its flavor must be compatible with that of the filler and the wrapper.

The **wrapper** is the proverbial cover by which the book is judged. The wrapper must be aesthetically pleasing, well-veined, even textured, and pleasant to the touch, or the chances of selling the cigar are seriously diminished. But that is not all. The wrapper can account for up to sixty percent of the a cigar's taste, so it has to be one fine leaf, well chosen to complement and enhance the contributions of the filler and the binder. The artistry required to apply the wrapper belongs to the roller, the most skilled craftsman in the cigar factory hierarchy.

Given the three components, there are still three ways in which they can be assembled to produce different types of cigars. Handmade cigars, true to their name, have each step of their construction completed by hand labor. In machine-bunched cigars, the filler is bunched (formed) by a machine, but the wrapper is applied by hand. For totally machine-made cigars, mechanical operations take care of all phases of the process.

The production of handmade cigars is blessedly old-fashioned in the best sense of the word. Pride in craftsmanship is not an antique phrase in a cigar factory, it is the underpinning of a century-old enterprise. A handmade cigar begins in the hands of the "buncher," who forms the filler into a cylindrical shape. Of course, this procedure is not accomplished the easy way, by rolling the leaves or folding them like a book. Instead the tobacco is crimped together like a fan to create horizontal air spaces for a good draw, and to ensure that when the cigar is smoked, each puff fuses all the tobacco flavors from the beginning to the end. The filler is rolled in a binder leaf and becomes a "bunch," a cigar naked of its wrapper. Bunches are placed about ten in a row, in wooden molds the size of the intended final product. The molds are stacked in a bunch press, which applies just enough squeeze to coax the bunches into the shape of cigars. During this scrunching time, up to forty-five minutes, the bunches are regularly rotated to create the expected cylindrical contour.

And on to the deft touch of the "roller," the elite, most skillful member of the cigar-making community. The expert roller trims the wrapper leaf to size, and encircles the cigar so that the leaf tip is at the foot and the leaf base is at the head. That way the milder flavor of the tobacco is in the smoker's first puffs. He then cuts a small piece for the cap and affixes it to the head with a sticky dab of natural tree gum. Anyone who aspires to become a master roller, a *torcedor*, must begin as an apprentice for two years. The few who graduate into this noble corps then labor for at least another six years before becoming proficient in all shapes. Standards are so rigorous that twenty years is not considered too long to become a master roller.

At this point in the process, the human role part becomes secondary, and nature takes command once again. The completed cigars, whose tobacco had been moistened so that it could be handled, are left on their own to dry in temperature-controlled cedar rooms. But drying is not all that occurs in these aging rooms. The flavors or each tobacco, so carefully chosen to complement one another, must have time to meld, to "marry," so that the individual tastes become nuances and the combined, singular character of the cigar comes to the fore. This sequestering lasts for a minimum of three weeks, but can be prolonged, for special series of cigars, for several months or even more than a year.

Complete at last, the cigars are subjected to still one more close examination, and then divided very specifically by color to be boxed. Each box must contain only cigars of exactly the same shade, a factor that is not related to taste or quality or consistency. It is a matter

of pride. A perfect box is a representation of the extra-ordinary care that has gone into the entire process of creating a handmade cigar.

Still, handmade cigars are not the only good ones. A machine-bunched and handrolled cigar is not a hands-*off* cigar, because while a machine turns out the bunch, a roller still applies the wrapper leaf and the cigars are inspected, sorted, and aged with care. Legally, these cigars can still be called handmade, and the machine-bunching process may actually be a benefit, since it guarantees consistency. Uneven results and human error, ever-present possibilities with handwork, can be avoided with machines. In addition, machine-bunched cigars are far less expensive than handmade ones, not at all an inconsequential factor.

Cigars made completely by machine are generally the province of the low-priced, mass market category. They are often made with homogenized tobacco leaf (HTL), a pulplike material consisting of tobacco stems and fibers mixed with a substance similar to cellulose. Often produced in sheets, homogenized tobacco leaf can be used for both binder and wrapper. ["Mass" is not just the word for the marketing of these cigars, for they are also produced in massive quantities by speed-demon machines.] Machine-made cigars are, by definition, the most consistent of all, and they are truly mild, a choice that may be perfect for those who smoke several cigars a day.

There are machine-made cigars that are *not* mass market, and they are some of the most popular in the world. These are the Dutch-type European cigars made by brands such as Christian of Denmark, Schimel-penninck, and Villiger. Some of these "dry" cigars are all tobacco, while others use homogenized leaf binder and wrapper. Generally they are machine bunched and use short filler, because they fall into the small cigar category. That does not mean that a dry cigar cannot be excellent. They are found in the repertoire of discriminating smokers, and some connoisseurs prefer these cigars exclusively.

HUMIDORS:
The Well-Kept Cigar

To smoke is human;
to smoke cigars is divine.

Anonymous

Some valuables, like paintings and jewelry, are meant to be displayed and worn, but cigars, perhaps the most precious of all, must be kept in the closet. Well, not actually in the closet, but certainly in a dark place without fluctuation in the climate. That means a humidor or any reasonable facsimile that your budget allows. Cigars should be stored at a temperature of 68-70 degrees and 70-72 percent humidity. This recreation of the tropical climate of the tobacco's first home keeps cigars from becoming dry and brittle, extends their lives, and even supplies an environment for "aging," if that is desirable. It is not that cigars are temperamental, they are simply botanical and cannot survive under conditions that would be harmful to the plant they once were. Hence the humidor.

Providing a constant source of humidity and air tightness is the humidor's role. You can even coddle cigars in a plastic container as long as you add a dampened paper towel or sponge (sealed in its own plastic bag). You can buy devices that are humidity regulators designed for large and small humidors. All humidors, even the most expensive, have humidifying elements that require water at regular intervals. Distilled water is preferable because some of these mechanisms can be damaged by the chemicals in tap water, which can also encourage mold in cigars. Mold can also get a grip if you let water come in direct contact with your cigars. Never do. Cigars are creatures of steady habits, so the humidifying element must not be too wet or too dry. Even those that have somehow missed your attention and dried out are not lost. They can always be rehumidified, but like a good smoke, the process cannot be hurried. They must rest for awhile in the humidifier as far away from the source of moisture as possible. (Any abrupt change is anathema to a cigar's nature).

Keeping cigars in a cedar box is often recommended because the wood imparts a spiciness that enhances the taste as cigars mature. If you keep cigars in this way, slip off the cellophane wrappers so that the natural mingling of flavors can occur. Cedar abets a process in which the various tobaccos in a cigar are said to "marry," that is merge into a more complex blend rather than remain separate in their individual flavors. This sharing of air forbids the addition of any flavored cigars. A few cedar strips can be added to plastic containers to upgrade those more mundane surroundings closer to the level of a cedar box.

If you buy a humidor, you are spending some wisely invested money, for the enjoyment you reap in well-kept cigars will be just compensation. Look for a humidor that will hold a practical number of the size of cigars you wish to keep. Beware of the fact that a humidor that claims to hold fifty cigars may be counting on smaller sizes than what you have in mind. Take care to examine the *inside* dimensions. Some humidors are lined with cedar, which is a matter of taste. There are those who believe that cedar, which absorbs humidity, competes with the cigars for moisture, thereby negating the positive aspects of the wood. Like many purchases, humidors can offer a bewildering number of options, so personal impulse is as good a guide as any.

The cost of a humidor ranges due to these many variables. They can be a few dollars or thousands. In April 1996, Sotheby's auctioned off millions of dollars worth of valuables from the estate of Jacqueline Kennedy Onassis. Among the esteemed pieces was a humidor belonging to President John F. Kennedy. The humidor went to Marvin R. Shanken, the highest bidder, for $574,500.

A humidor's outside construction should feature a piano hinge and a firmly closing lid, one that is well-balanced and will not tip the box when opened. As prices increase, so do the possibilities, so you will find humidors with levels and trays and locks and handles and finishes that rival handcrafted cabinets. Some offer hygrometers which measure the level of humidity, a device that can also be purchased separately. When the enjoyment of your smoking begins with the opening of your humidor, you are ready to own one that adds to the ambiance of your total experience.

Certainly, you would not want to open your refrigerator for a cigar, a place that is sometimes mentioned for storage. Frost-free refrigerators have the most negative effect of all—removing moisture—so they are hardly the place to protect cigars. There is one time when your freezer/refrigerator can be used, and that is in the battle against the tobacco worm. Despite fumigating during cigar processing, the eggs of these creatures sometimes lay dormant in a cigar. If they hatch in the ripe atmosphere of your humidor, they can cause havoc. If this dreaded situation occurs, examine all the cigars for the boring hole this beetle makes, and discard those that have been attacked. Seal the rest in a plastic bag and put them in the freezer for a few days to kill all possible reinfestations. Then let them rest in the refrigerator for several more days before returning them to room temperature. The gradual change in climate is vital or the wrappers will split and your salvation effort will be for naught. Clean the humidor thoroughly so it will once again be a safe haven for your cigars.

Marvin R. Shanken, Editor and Publisher,
Cigar Aficionado Magazine *with the JFK Humidor.*

Another blight that can unfortunately occur is mold—green, blue, and ugly as such monsters tend to be. The cigars that are affected have to be sacrificed and, again, the humidor has to be completely cleaned and aerated. A grayish, white dusting sometimes occurs on a cigar's wrapper. This is *plume* or *bloom*, a sign of oils exuding from the cigar as it ages. Simply wipe it with a soft cloth.

While your cigars are so well cared for at home, you may obviously want to smoke them elsewhere. In that regard, you need a carrying case, since cigars are too likely to be bent or crushed when traveling unprotected. The important thing is that the case fit whatever cigars you regularly enjoy. Long cigars require a telescoping case. Cigars of the same ring gauge can use a fingered case. Consider how many cigars you will carry and whether they are likely to be loose in the case, and select one in which they will not knock against one another. Examine a leather case for rough spots that could tear a cigar. Remember that a four-fingered case will not fit in your pocket. Never put a partially smoked cigar in a case with others because its aroma will permeate them all. And return unsmoked cigars that you are carrying to your humidor on a daily basis. A case will not keep them fresh, only a traveling humidor will do that, and, yes, you can buy one of those, too. Maintaining your cigars in the best possible condition is hardly a chore. It is a merely a way of expressing consideration for one of the best companions you can have at home or on the road.

CHOOSING A CIGAR:
The Art of Selection

As concerns tobacco, there are many superstitions.
And the chiefest is this—that there is a standard governing
the matter, whereas there is nothing of the kind.
Each man's preference is the only standard for him,
the only one which he can accept, the only one which can
command him. A congress of all the tobacco-lovers
in the world could not elect a standard which
would be binding upon you or me, or would
even much influence us.

Mark Twain
"Concerning Tobacco," 1893

I t is an axiom of cigar smoking that there is no perfect cigar. There is only the right cigar for you, the
one that gratifies your taste buds and sense of smell.
The joy of searching for the best cigar is in the journey
itself—one smoke at a time. The devilish number of
different cigars makes choosing one seem like picking a
winning lottery number, but with a little knowledge and
curiosity, you can embark on a quest that is its own
reward.

The Brand
The information you need begins with the brands,
some of which have a problem of double identity that
stems from the Cuban revolution in 1959. When Castro
came to power and nationalized the tobacco industry,
many of the manufacturers fled—and believed they
could take their brand names with them. The Cubans
who remained disagreed, and continued to produce cigars with the original names. Today, there are still brands
such as Romeo y Julieta, Montecristo, Partagas, Punch,
and others that are actually made by two different companies, one in Cuba and the other elsewhere in the
Caribbean. The mark of a Cuban brand is on the band,
where "Havana" is written in miniature.

The Color
The battalions of cigars lined up on tobacconists

shelves speak first with the color of their wrappers. Growers perceive over sixty hues, but smokers limit the confusion to about seven. In general, the lighter the color, the milder the taste; the darker the shade, the sweeter and more full-bodied the flavor. The following is a list that nature does not strictly adhere to:

Claro Claro ● This greenish-tinted wrapper also goes by the names of *double claro, candela, jade,* and A.M.S. for "American Market Selection" because of its former popularity in the United States. It produces a very mild, even bland taste.

Claro ● A light, yellowish tan leaf preferred for its neutral flavor.

Colorado Claro ● A tawny, light brown with a light flavor.

Colorado ● A reddish-brown to brown hue. With its rich flavor and subtle aroma, this wrapper is called E.M.S. for "English Market Selection" because it was previously prized in Europe, but is now equally desirable in the United States.

Colorado Maduro ● Medium brown in color and medium strength.

Maduro ● Black coffee describes this wrapper and gives a good indication of the strength of its flavor. It is also known as S.M.S. for "Spanish Market Selection."

Oscuro ● The nearly black color of this leaf is darker than any other, because it is left the longest to mature on the tobacco plant and undergoes a lengthier curing period.

The Origin of the Tobacco

How much of the cigar's total character is affected by the wrapper is a matter of opinion, but there is no question that the impact is considerable. Still, the bulk of a cigar is in its body, the filler, and the blend of tobaccos in the filler should be considered when choosing a cigar. The filler's character depends upon the tobacco's country of origin. The major premium tobacco/cigar producing locations are: Cuba, Brazil, the Dominican Republic, Honduras, Jamaica, Sumatra, the

Philippines, the Canary Islands, Cameroon, Ecuador, Holland, Mexico, Nicaragua, and the United States, where Connecticut shade-wrapper leaf, the finest in the world, is grown. The following list, without accounting for the vagaries of particular weather conditions and crops, offers a very general impression of what the different growing venues might contribute to the overall taste:

Dominican Republic • By far the most popular cigars in the United States, these tend to be mild, with a sweet, nut-like taste. Earthy and floral tones are common.

Honduras • Cigars that are more robust and spicier than Dominicans. Nearly as rich as tobacco from Cuba.

Havana • Considered the best in the world, Havana cigars are medium to full-bodied, with earthy, coffee, and honeyed tones. Havana is also used as part of the blend in European dry cigars.

Jamaica • Jamaican cigars, of which the most famous is Macanudo, are a bit milder than Dominicans.

Nicaragua • Nicaraguans, which are improving, are medium sweet, full-bodied and aromatic.

Ecuador • Ecuadorian cigars are mild and flavorful.

Cameroon • A leaf, not a cigar, this wrapper imparts a spicy taste and a sharp aroma.

Sumatra • Also a tobacco, not a cigar, this Indonesian variety tends to be mild, but still spicy.

Mexico • Still a premium cigar, but one with an unpredictable spectrum from mild to heavy.

Brazil • Tobacco and cigars from Brazil tend to be dark, rich, and smooth with a slightly sweet flavor.

The Shape

Filled, wrapped, and rolled, a cigar presents itself in an array of bodies whose differences are defined by fractions of inches. There are so many different sizes and shapes of cigars now that, stood on end, they would resemble a miniature jungle of short, tall, irregular, and stately trees. Like the natural world, the products of the cigar industry are not much given to uniformity. At one time, cigars of a given name such as a Churchill were a standard size. No longer. Today, a "Churchill" can range anywhere from 6¾ to 8 inches and the same loose association between name and dimensions occurs in all sizes.

Cigars are described by their length in inches and their diameter, called the "ring gauge," which is measured in 64ths of an inch. So a cigar designated 6½ x 46 is six-and-a-half inches long and just under three-quarters of an inch (48/64) in diameter. The Europeans use millimeters and measure the circumference of the cigar rather than the diameter. Thus the 6½ x 46 becomes 165mm x 18.26mm. Because names and dimensions do not coincide uniformly, it is best to explore a preferred size no matter what the manufacturer chooses to call it.

Regardless of length and girth, there are two basic types of cigars, the *parejos*, cigars with straight sides, and the *figuardos*, those with irregular shapes.

Although the distinctions can be finer than those on the following list, the straight-sided cigars fall into these categories:

Corona • This cigar, with its aristocratic title (Spanish for *crown*), is the traditional benchmark by which all other sizes are measured. Its medium size, 5½ to 6 inches by 42 or 44 is adaptable to most occasions and offers at least 45 minutes of pleasurable smoking. Like most straight-sided cigars, the corona has an open foot and a closed head.

Churchill • At least 7 x 47, the Churchill is a strong, full-bodied cigar that takes its character from its namesake, Winston Churchill, who probably smoked more of them in a single lifetime than anyone else on the planet.

Double Corona • From the more-is-better school of thought, this cigar, at approximately 6 ½ x 48, offers ample girth for well-blended tobaccos and full flavor.

Petit Corona • As its name implies, this is a smaller cigar, ranging from 5" to 5 ½" with ring gauges of 38–44, ideal for a briefer smoke.

Panatela • These cigars are generally longer and thinner than coronas. The slenderness offers less space for tobacco and a coinciding drop in complexity of flavors. In addition, a smaller ring gauge burns hotter than a larger one.

Lonsdale • These are the One-From-Column-A-and-One-From-Column-B cigars. They are thicker than panatelas and longer than coronas.

Rothschild • Here is a cigar with heft and brevity. Short but with a capacious 50 ring gauge, a Rothschild is a very substantial smoke.

The irregular *figuardos* are the stand-out personalities in the tobacco trade. Each has idiosyncrasies that add a particular quality to the smoking experience. The foot or head on these cigars may be open or closed, pointed or rounded. They may look amusing but they are found in the humidors of serious smokers. Some of the major shapes of *figuardos*, which may occur with variations, are as follows:

Perfecto • Once more popular, now almost a caricature, the perfecto is tapered at both ends with a bulge at its midsection.

Torpedo • A cigar with the name and shape of a weapon, the torpedo has a pointed head, closed foot, and middle bulge.

Pyramid • This cigar has a pointed closed head and an open, widened foot which makes for a memorable first puff.

Diadema • A grandiose 8 inches or larger with a ring gauge of at least 60, this monster is straight-walled with a rounded head and, most often, an open foot.

Culebra • "Snake" in Spanish, the culebra is a triple threat, three long, thin cigars braided together. The pointed heads are separate and they are meant to be smoked individually.

Bellicoso • At 5 $\frac{1}{2}$ inches with a ring gauge of 52, this cigar has comparative girth and a shaped neck that is easy to clip.

The Dry

To add another dimension, think *small* and *dry*, two attributes that none of the above cigars offer and might seem undesirable. But the diminutive European "Dutch-type" cigars are another interesting variety of smoke with some advantages. Sold in packs of several sizes, they are portable and easy to stash in a pocket or drawer. Because they require no humidification, they can go on the road for any period of time. Ideal for brief interludes, these "dry" cigars are available in a wide range of blends from light and mild to dark and rich.

The Best

Of course, in all these types and shapes, there are some cigars considered to be better quality than others. In general, the most popular cigars among serious smokers are *premium* cigars, made with long leaf filler tobacco. These are mostly handmade, but they can also be machine bunched and handrolled. Stepping up a grade, there are also *super-premium* cigars, which are distinguished by specially selected tobaccos in the filler blend and the wrapper, and additional aging. Moving into an even more rarefied realm, there are *vintage* cigars which, like wine, are made exclusively from a single year's outstanding tobacco crop. With their own bands and boxes, vintage cigars are marketed with all the cachet of exclusivity.

The Purchase

Armed in your quest for the right cigar with some knowledge about the color, filler, and shape, you are prepared to take a cigar in hand and inspect it carefully. Appearance and condition count. You may never be Sherlock Holmes, who could identify a cigar by its ash, but you can consider the clues the wrapper offers. A worm hole, of course, eliminates any candidate. The color should be even, without blotches, but sunspots are permissible. Although a cigar should not be heavily veined, veins in the leaf are part of tobacco's distinct character and often announce its origin. Cameroon wrapper, for example, has more evident veins than Connecticut leaf. To the touch, Cameroon wrapper feels bumpy, but this texture, called "tooth," is, in this leaf, a harbinger of a good-tasting cigar. On the other hand, fine Connecticut wrapper has a smoother surface texture and less tooth. Any wrapper with an oily sheen is announcing that it has been properly cured and humidified. At seventy percent humidity, tobacco secretes oil and may feel almost silky to the touch. A cigar that is dry or brittle, or shows cracks along the wrapper, is unacceptable.

How a cigar feels is part of its résumé, so do take it in hand, tenderly (by the foot, not the head, so as not to injure the cap), and check for any hard or soft spots that might be evidence of a poorly constructed filler that would influence the draw. A cigar's weight may indicate how tightly or loosely it is packed and whether it will be an easy draw, which is a matter of personal choice. Since test tasting is not part of the negotiation in buying a cigar, your search has, at this point, reached the point of purchase. Take the plunge.

Buying cigars is an adventure no matter how experienced you are, but even in the beginning you may want to buy more than one. An opportunity for acquiring several at a better price is the "bundle," usually five cigars packaged together. Although you cannot inspect each individually, the better-quality bundles are, indeed, very good. Cigars are also sold in boxes, of twenty or twenty-five, and can be less expensive in that form. Check the box carefully to make sure that all the members are the same color, a sign of attention on the part of the manufacturer.

Some styles of packaging are indicated by a cigar's name. For example, an "8-9-8" moniker means that the cigars are arranged in a round-sided box in three rows, eight on the bottom, nine in the middle and eight on top. *Amatista* is a term that refers to a glass jar with fifty cigars. Then there are the *tubos*, individual cigars packed in tightly sealed aluminum, glass, or wooden tubes. While the search for the perfect cigar is a lifelong treasure quest, these easy-to-carry singles are perfect in their own way, ever ready for any time that might be the right moment for a cigar.

CUTTING THE CIGAR:
The Opening Act

*I have made it a rule
never to smoke more than
one cigar at a time.*

Mark Twain

on his seventieth birthday, having been told to limit his cigars

---

Any act of satisfying pleasure has preparatory rituals. Cigar smoking has many. First, there is anticipatory delight. Then there is the simple motion of taking the cigar in hand and engaging all the senses, rolling it gently with your fingers to feel its suppleness, its physicality. Relishing its color and shape. Inhaling its enticing bouquet unhurriedly. The time spent in these ceremonial moments is not just a prelude, but the initial step in the arc of your total satisfaction.

However, there are several things *not* to do at this time. There is no reason to remove the band which is, after all, part of the fine craftsmanship that distinguishes a cigar from more plebeian pastimes. In addition to aesthetic considerations, the band may be attached to the wrapper by a bit of glue, and slipping it off may damage the delicate wrapper. If you really want to take off the band, wait until the warmth of the heated cigar loosens the glue. Above all, resist the impulse, if it occurs, to lick the cigar. It is not an ice cream cone, which is an indulgence of an altogether different sort. This practice has its origins in pre-humidor days and is not only unnecessary now, but unsavory.

Participating in the joy of cigar smoking demands an openness to new possibilities and a few technical skills. They begin with the cut, the opening that must be made in the head of all premium cigars. That cut should not be unkind, but a clean one that respects the delicacy with which the cap has been applied to the head. A good cut allows the cigar to draw properly. The choices are a "guillotine" cut, a straight line across the head, a "V cut," a V-shaped wedge cut into the head, or a "pierce," which is a hole punched into the center of the head. The instruments for this small, intimate act of

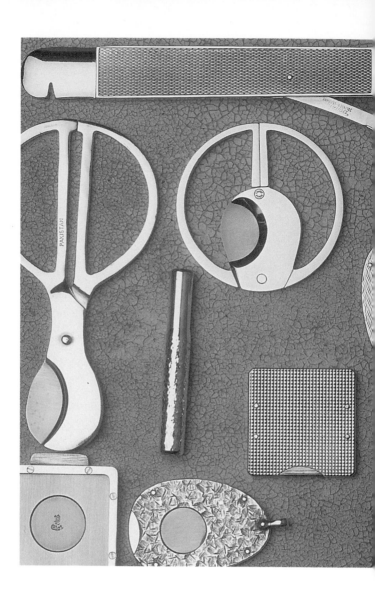

violence are the guillotine, the notch cutter, and the piercer. Cuts can also be made with a specially designed cigar scissors or a less lofty but always handy penknife. Whatever your weapon, the ideal cut is a restrained one. If you infringe upon the point where the cap connects to the wrapper, the cigar will unravel and a fuzzy ended cigar is an unpalatable one. To be safe, always cut above this line.

The guillotine, with its attendant images of brutal beheadings, actually produces the most gentle and civilized of cuts. A quick review of the other instruments reveals its practicality.

The notch cutter does provide a cut with two surface sides that should produce a good draw. But few of these blades cut without leaving ragged edges. And they work poorly on tapered or pointed heads. In addition, they are not adequate for larger ring sizes and are nearly impossible to sharpen. The piercer creates a hole, not a cut, and therein lies its difficulty. The single hole can concentrate rancid acids and tobacco juices and aim them inauspiciously at your tongue. When the cigar is pierced, tobacco may pack against the sides and bottom of the hole, affecting the draw. For all of the above reasons, piercers are no longer in vogue. There are cigar scissors, but these take some expertise to use and cutting a wedge with a knife requires scalpel-like precision, lest the cut amputate rather than open. Finally, deftly pinching the cap with a fingernail is the most accessible method, but it takes nimble fingers to create the sought-after source through which the soul of a cigar will emerge.

The size of the cut is as important as the dimensions of the cigar you choose. It affects the taste, the draw, the length of the smoke, and, obviously, the quality of your experience. An opening that is too large will produce a *whoosh* of smoke into your mouth, an excess of heat, and a bitter taste. Your cigar will smoke too fast, which may be just as well, because the time spent on this cigar will be largely wasted. However, an opening that is too small has other unappetizing properties. The draw will be difficult, the actual amount of smoke minimal, and. the taste ruined by a concentration of tars and nicotine. The ideal cut is slightly smaller than the diameter of the cigar. A guillotine generally completes the task quickly and admirably.

The guillotine, which looks and operates just like its namesake, makes a clean, level, round opening at the end of a cigar, facilitating an easy draw and full flavor. Inexpensive plastic guillotines are readily portable, and last several months. There are better-quality models such as the Paul Gamarian Cigar Cutter, which has a Sheffield steel blade. And a two-bladed model such as the Portable Zino Cigar Cutter by Davidoff has the advantage of a faster, cleaner cut. Whatever instrument you choose, remember that a dull blade will demolish your cigar. The swift, precise snip is the object of every guillotine, whether it is the one that fueled the French Revolution, or the one that unlocks the pleasures of your cigar.

LIGHTING THE CIGAR:
The Slow Burn

*Do not ask me to describe the charms
of reverie, or the contemplative ecstasy into which
the smoke of our cigar plunges us.*

Jules Sandeau
French novelist

Toasting with a drink is a act of celebration. Lighting a cigar is a toast in this sense, too, but it is also an actual "toasting" of the cigar's foot. In the proper lighting of a cigar, *the flame never touches the cigar.* The way you light a cigar affects how it will taste and how it will burn, so lighting up correctly is paramount. The best lighters are butane because of their colorless, odorless fuel. Long cedar wood smokers' matches are another good option. Never choose a kerosene lighter or a cardboard match impregnated with chemicals, for they will despoil the treasure.

With a cigar in one hand and a lighter in the other, you enter into a ritual that all smokers share. If you strike a match, pause until the flame has burned away the sulfur, then begin. *Never* submerge the foot of the cigar in the flame. This verboten act will turn the tobacco to carbon, the cooked, burnt taste of which will be with you from the first draw to the last. And never begin with the cigar in your mouth. Hold it in your hand, about a quarter of an inch above the flame, at a 45 degree angle. Rotate the cigar slowly so that the rim of the foot is lightly and evenly toasted and the filler begins to dry out.

Toasting is a gentle art that requires patience and a caring eye to make sure that the entire rim is lit. If the whole circumference is not evenly warmed, the cigar will not smoke evenly. If one side burns faster than the other, a condition called "tunneling" occurs, and the cigar will never smoke properly. When you see the ash encircling the wrapper and wisps of smoke begin rising, bring the cigar to your lips, gently puff, rotating it directly over (but not in) the tip of the flame in order to light the entire outer circle. If the cigar is well lit, the

first long puff will be the most full flavored and satisfying of all. Savor it.

From time to time, even a well-lit cigar can go out in midsmoke. If that should happen, gently knock off the ash and check to see if the fire is truly gone by exhaling through the cigar very carefully. If no smoke appears, first warm the end of the cigar, rotating it over a flame to release the tars, then relight. As you relight the edges of the wrapper, you may find the whole cigar burning again. A relit cigar may smoke stronger, but it is better by far than no cigar at all.

Lighting a cigar, from striking the flame to taking the first puff, is one of the most intimate ceremonial aspects of cigar smoking. The quality of the transition from anticipation to participation depends upon the skill, concentration, and delicacy with which the act is performed. It is a moment when the smoker demonstrates respect and appreciation, and the cigar responds to that attention. It is a moment of truly private pleasure.

THE SKILLFUL SMOKER:
Maximizing the Pleasure

*To know how to smoke is to recover
certain forgotten rhythms, to re-establish
communication with the self.*

Zino Davidoff

Savoring a cigar is often compared to enjoying a fine wine. Indeed, cigar connoisseurs speak of "sipping" the flavor of the smoke. The analogy is an apt one, for taste buds are the keenest conduits of a cigar's pleasures. Relishing the complexity and serendipitous combinations of flavors in cigar smoke is comparable to the delight found in an excellent wine or a gourmet meal. Of course, appreciation does take proper smoking and some practice.

Rule one is that cigar smokers never inhale. Simply hold the smoke in your mouth for a delicious moment

Laurence Sherman lighting a cigar

and then exhale and watch the smoke rise. The smoke is not a by-product, but the key to the pleasure. A cigar's taste and aroma are borne in the smoke as it enters and exits the mouth, leaving its taste behind—spicy, nutty, woody, rich, or light, an undefinable hint of earthiness, a touch of the sublime—a sensation that cannot be captured in words but only in smoke, the most ephemeral of all substances.

Puffing should never be hurried, but must occur at about one minute intervals to keep the cigar lit. Of course, a certain attention is required to keep this duet between you and your cigar in rhythm. And the tempo should be measured: the faster one smokes, the less pleasurable the experience. Puffing like a chimney is not only inelegant but contrary to the purpose of cigar smoking, which is essentially a contemplative pleasure. In addition, puffing too often will cause the cigar to overheat and create a harsh flavor. As Auguste Barthelmy wrote in *L'Art de Fume Pipe & Cigare* (1849) "The true smoker abstains from imitating Vesuvius." Precisely.

A gently puffed cigar will provide forty-five minutes or more of enjoyment, during which time it is best to keep the head of the cigar as dry as possible. That means it should not be resting in your mouth. A wet cigar not only looks offensive, but will begin to taste poorly as tars and nicotine collect in the saliva. Hold the cigar firmly in your mouth when puffing, but do not clench it. During the entire time that you are smoking, the cigar should only be in your mouth for about three minutes. You should be savoring the flavor, not tasting wet tobacco.

Once you become sensitive to the nuances of flavor, it becomes obvious that the first half of a cigar is not the same as the second. The taste changes as the length of the cigar diminishes. The smoke intensifies as the tobacco grows shorter and somewhere along the way— every cigar is different—the taste will turn, and not for the better. Most cigars, no matter what their grade, will pass their peak when they have been smoked to about one-third of their length. Some connoisseurs prefer to abandon the smoke before it reaches that point. Most experienced cigar smokers recognize when the cigar has given its true essence and put it down with satisfaction. Some people never give up. However, a cigar whose taste has intensified to sourness will leave an unpleasant remembrance in your mouth, and an odor in the room that will justify all the complaints of those who find smoking objectionable. The extra puffs, after the cigar signals its demise, are usually not that enjoyable and probably not worth the consequences.

During its all too brief but lovely life, a cigar does leave behind a footprint—its ash. A cigar that is burning properly will produce a long, firm ash. A flaky ash is not only a sign of insufficiency, but is also likely to be messy. Cigar culture has promulgated the notion that the best-quality cigars will produce a white ash. White may be aesthetically pleasing, but it is, for the most part, irrelevant. The fine sight of an inch of ash is an indication of a well-constructed cigar and, at that point, it should be watched to insure that the ash falls naturally and gracefully into an ashtray. "Tipping" the ash, if it becomes too long, can be encouraged by a long puff to heat up the foot and a light, sharp tap in the ashtray. The ideal result is a neat break, revealing a foot with the glow of a well-heated cigar.

The ashtray should be a cigar's final resting place. Permitting a cigar to burn itself out, which it will do quickly, will produce the least odor. Crushing it out only increases the exposed tobacco and so the unpleasant fumes. A spent, cold cigar does have a smell that could never be called a fragrance, and so it is best not to leave it in the trash indoors at all, if possible.

Even though cigar smoking is far more ideal than life in general, there are times when the course of events do go awry. Sometimes a cigar simply will not draw well, a difficulty that may be caused when the bunching is too tight. Called a "tight draw," it has reduced taste and a tendency to extinguish. The filler may even contain a knot or "plug" that blocks the passage of smoke. On the other hand, a "loose draw," a cigar that is underfilled, risks burning and harshness because too much smoke will come through too quickly. Finally, a cigar may burn too quickly and unevenly down one side of the wrapper, a condition that may be the result of poor construction or inadequate humidification. Despite heroic attempts at resuscitation, these situations are usually hopeless. The best course is to lay your disappointments on the counter of the tobacconist who sold them to you. Most good merchants will offer credit. But for the moment, light up another, because the time set aside for a cigar is only wasted on anything else.

The humidor behind the bar at
Granville Restaurant and Lounge.

THE TIME AND PLACE
TO SMOKE:
An Hour of One's Own

He who doth not smoke hath either known no great
griefs, or refuseth himself the softest consolation,
next to that which comes from heaven.

E.G. Bulwer-Lytton

"Gentlemen, you may smoke," King Edward VII proclaimed on the day he assumed the English throne. And joyful courtiers, free at last from years of stern dissuasion from Edward's mother, Queen Victoria, lit their cigars. True smokers look forward to every cigar with that much anticipation.

For most smokers, cigars are a passion, not just a diversion. When and where and what they smoke is a planned, not spontaneous occasion. One reason is that it takes time to adequately smoke a cigar, an event that deserves full attention. And the time may be considerable. A corona takes at least thirty minutes, perhaps more, and a churchill can take close to an hour. Beginners are often urged to select smaller cigars at first because of their milder flavor and shorter duration, and this advice has merit. However, the larger ring

sizes do tend to smoke more smoothly because they heat up less quickly, so personal preference and lifestyle must be your guides. But, whatever you choose, the first rule is to allow the time necessary to do justice to the cigar. A cigar demands that and you deserve it.

No one but the Mexican lord of machismo, Pancho Villa, ever suggested on record that a cigar is a good idea before breakfast, but at almost any other time of the day your taste buds are well enough prepared if you are so inclined. Most people prefer lighter and milder cigars earlier in the day. After lunch is an agreeable

time for a cigar, especially if the cigar complements the food. A light lunch calls for a mild cigar; a more substantial meal, a full-flavored cigar. Most people do not have the leisure to enjoy a cigar in the afternoon, but again, lighter would be better to allow your taste buds time to recuperate before dinner. It is not unusual for the taste of the same cigar to vary according to the hour, your appetite, and your mental and physical condition at the moment. The alchemy of a cigar is in the interplay of the smoker and the smoke.

Prime time for a cigar is after the evening meal—the

hour for relaxation, for contemplation, for the interlude that reorders perspectives and renews spirits. Serious smokers would not find the word "meditation" inappropriate, for a satisfying cigar, and the pause in life's headlong thrust that is required to smoke it, creates a haven of quietude and introspection. Once these moments are an established part of your life they become more and more desirable, for, in addition to being a great pleasure, they are a key to the refreshment of your inner resources.

In contrast to these private moments, there are purely convivial places to smoke cigars. "Smoker Nights" at restaurants are a growing phenomenon. There is nothing quite like an atmosphere of like-minded souls bonding in a haze of fine smoke, food and drink. And the ultimate cigar social settings are clubs like Hamilton's (as in George) in Beverly Hills, and Club Macanudo in New York where you can rent a humidor, nibble on delicacies prepared by a celebrity chef, and even conduct business if you must fit that into your schedule.

In private, or in public, alone or with friends, where and when you prefer to smoke is as personal as your favorite cigar. The only common denominator is that, no matter what the choice, a cigar is always an excellent companion.

CIGAR BOXES:
The Fine Print

*What this country needs
is a good five cent cigar.*

Thomas Marshall
U.S. Vice President, 1919

The Connoisseur's Book of the Cigar is a contemplation of cigars written by Zino Davidoff,
founder of the cigar empire that bears his name. The
book's cover replicates a cedar cigar box complete with
colorful label and edging designs. The light-heartedness
of the packaging belies the work's rather erudite tone,
but the contrast is fitting. The book has the look of an
old-fashioned gift, which is just what a box of cigars is.
The serious pleasure is on the inside.

Most premium cigars are boxed in cedar, which
enhances the cigars' flavors and helps prevent drying.
Boxes come in two versions, the cedar plywood "dress
box," which is blanketed with labels and edging
designs, and the cedar "cabinet box," which is outfitted
with brass hinges and nails that will not rust in the
humidity of a tobacconist's humidor. Since the nineteenth century, manufacturers have been applying orna-
mental labels to boxes in much the same way as today.
Imposing personages, alluring ladies, enticing planta-
tions, crossed-sword insignias, and all sorts of dramatic
images beautify cigar boxes as if the contents were a
precious offering—which, in fact, they are. But some of
the papering is not merely decorative. On Cuban cigars,
once the box is nailed shut, a green and white label is
applied to indicate that the product is genuine Havana.
Following this custom, similar marks of brand authen-
ticity are added by many companies.

With that in mind, it is important to be aware of the
true signs of cigars made in Cuba. Before Castro came
to power, the underside of the box was stamped with
"Made in Havana—Cuba" If you buy a box of cigars
with this stamp, they should be pre-embargo. After
1961, this inscription was replaced with *Hecho en
Cuba*. In 1985 Cubatabaco's logo was added with a fac-

tory code, but in 1994 that mark was replaced with *Habanos SA*.

But no matter where the cigars are made, the box should tell you *how* they are made. Only *Totalmente a mano* means completely handmade, and the cigars will be priced accordingly. Beyond that, there is some confusion. *Hecho a Mano*, or "Made by Hand," fails to specify exactly *how much* of the cigar was touched by human hands. Cigars that are machine bunched and hand finished may carry this label. They also may say

"Hand Rolled," which, again, means that only the wrapper was applied by hand. And further possibilities for deception lie in *Envuelto a mano*, which simply means hand-packed, not even close to handmade.

Thus, even in the genteel world of cigars, buyers must beware, or at the very least, informed. The intriguing designs, with their golden lions, handsome birds, and swirling script are one of the most delightful cigar traditions. But to know about the cigars, read the box.

JUDGING THE CIGAR:
Consistency Counts

*I am sure there are many things better
than a good cigar, but right now,
I can't think of what they might be.*

Richard Carleton Hacker
author, **The Ultimate Cigar Book**

Assume you have an all-natural tobacco, long filled, handmade cigar in hand. If anticipation is half the pleasure, you are already enjoying yourself. But total pleasure demands a cigar with certain characteristics, and being able to discern their quality is important in choosing your cigars. Judging a cigar's taste is subjective territory, and the verdict is yours alone. But in assessing a cigar's quality, definite standards and objective conclusions can be made.

There is only one standard in judging cigars: consistency, which, in all areas of life, is defined as being able to perform on a high level, time after time after time. So it is with cigars. Consistency is the hallmark of excellence, the common denominator for evaluating the two basic components of a cigar, construction and tobacco.

The measure of a cigar's construction is that it must draw and burn well, a consequence of the filling. If a cigar is underfilled, it will be an easy draw, which is sometimes considered an advantage. But if the draw is too easy, there will be a fast burn, causing unpleasant heat and harshness, a hot smoke. On the other hand, if a cigar is overfilled, it will be hard to draw, and may even have a plug—a dense area that makes for an impossible draw. With a hard draw, the volume of smoke is diminished and, with it, the amount of taste and aroma, the two crucial elements in a good cigar.

In addition to the draw, a cigar's construction should enable it to burn evenly all the way down, a sign of proper rolling. The ash should be firm and grow to an inch without falling. The mouth feel should be firm and resilient; a mushy cigar is neither pleasant nor well built. And the cigar in hand should give back a spring of liveliness. None of these are guarantees of a great cigar, but they are the fundamentals of construction and an educated appraisal.

In regard to tobacco, again, consistency is the benchmark. Obviously, the tobacco must be of a uniformly high quality and be processed properly. Beyond that, consistency in taste and aroma depends on the producer's ability to maintain an inventory of the tobaccos that go into the blends. Since tobacco growing is subject to the unpredictable misfortunes of weather and crop failure, a company must have a leaf supply that enables overlapping one crop to another for slow integration— which results in *consistency* in the blends.

A note of caution: One smoke of one type of cigar is not a reasonable test. How many you are willing to smoke of a single cigar to appraise its worth is subject to your time, temperament, and pocketbook. A box would be an equitable, but expensive assessment. But finally, given consistency in construction and tobacco, the test of how a cigar tastes and smells is purely personal. No one can tell another whether champagne or chardonnay, caviar or cabbage tastes better. So it is with cigars. The ultimate judgment rests in the opinion of the smoker.

STARS AND CIGARS:
A Smoking Fraternity

*The cigar is the perfect complement
to an elegant lifestyle.*

George Sand

In 1962, only hours before President Kennedy decreed the Cuban embargo, he dispatched an aide to secure a personal supply of one thousand H. Upmann Petit Coronas. General Ulysses S. Grant, a chain cigar smoker, would have understood. So would United States Senator Henry Clay, whose passion for cigars is immortalized in a brand that still bears his name.

If you smoke cigars, you are in good company. Consider Albert Einstein and Sigmund Freud, two great minds: one probed the universe, the other our inner world, and both smoked cigars. The range of geniuses stretches from the sublime (Maurice Ravel created ethereal music in the inspiring haze of cigar smoke) to the raucous (Babe Ruth smoked prodigiously and had his picture on the wrapper of a nickel cigar). History reveals extraordinary cigar smokers. The one without peer is the man who wielded his cigar and rallied his country with the force of his personality, Winston Churchill. First exposed to cigars at twenty-two when he was garrisoned in Cuba during the Spanish-American War, Churchill is said to have smoked over a quarter of a million cigars by the time of his death at ninety-one—about four thousand a year. His favorite, from his humidified room of three thousand, was a 48-ring gauge double corona, the cigar that became his namesake. He always chose maduros.

The only colossal cigar smoker to outlive Churchill was George Burns, who began smoking at fourteen and put down his last smoke right after his one hundredth birthday. An El Producto Queen was his beloved sidekick in private and on stage. Burns shared his cigar signature with Groucho Marx who had three famous trademarks—his mustache, his eyebrows, and a gargantuan cigar, which he used to smooth out the rough edges of his act. "If you forget a line," he once said, "all you

*Bill Cosby achieving celebrity cigar
status on the cover of Cigar Aficionado.*

have to do is stick the cigar in your mouth and puff on it until you can think of what you've forgotten." His on-camera cigars were never lit, but Groucho was a two-cigar-a-day-man with a penchant for Dunhill 410s.

Edward G. Robinson can also be found in the cigar-as-prop school, hustling his way to stardom as a gangster chewing on a stogie. And Charlie Chaplin displayed a cigar to symbolize the evil fat cat who oppressed the innocent downtrodden. Cigars have had their image problems, but not when the smoker is everyone's delight, Bill Cosby. Enjoying his cigars with contagious glee, Cosby makes smoking as all-American as basketball. He has not come late to cigars with wealth and celebrity, but learned to smoke as a youngster retreating to the basement with his grandfather for the pleasure of his company. Now he prefers a Hoyo de Monterrey double corona, which he says is his "favorite Cuban since Desi Arnaz."

Desi's wife Lucille Ball smoked cigarillos, which would not have surprised her fans who saw her as the wacky, try-anything Lucy she portrayed on television. But there is nothing silly about women smoking cigars, a pastime they enjoyed for centuries until the changing mores of nineteenth century western culture made smoking the exclusive preserve of men. The only woman of that period history offers as a cigar-smoking example is George Sand, the formidably independent writer who in 1867 gave us these marvelous words: "A cigar numbs sorrows and fills the solitary hours with a million gracious images."

Today the roster of women cigar smokers is legion and they are true connoisseurs: Madonna, Whoopi Goldberg, and Bette Midler like to light up. Supermodel Linda Evangelista smokes Cohiba panatelas and perennial model, actress, talk show host Lauren Hutton, who first smoked cigars with women in native villages while traveling, enjoys 41 ring size Dominican H. Upmanns. Both these women share their zest for cigars with their men, an arrangement once commented upon by the French writer Colette, who is rumored to have smoked in bed. "If a woman knows a man's preferences, including his preference in cigars," she said, "and if a man knows what a woman likes, they will be suitably armed to face one another."

Perhaps today Rudyard Kipling would enjoy the synergy between women and men and cigars and revise the line he wrote in 1886 in "The Betrothed," a poem anticipating the conflict between his bride and his beloved cigar: "A woman is only a woman, but a good cigar is a smoke" Fortunately, other cigar smoking literary giants have commented on cigars without reference to women. Somerset Maugham praised cigars as life's one true satisfaction, "the only realized ambition which has not brought disillusion" And the inimitable Mark Twain, who was often pictured with a cigar in hand, had this final word on where one should be allowed to smoke: "If I cannot smoke in heaven, then I shall not go."

More than likely Twain was there to welcome Jack Kennedy and apprise him of the celestial smoking rules. Back on earth, the Kennedy clan is carrying on the cigar-smoking tradition. Cigar aficionado Arnold Schwarzennegger is married to Kennedy's niece, Maria Shriver, and co-owns The Havana Room, a private Beverly Hills cigar club. Life goes on, and it goes better with a good cigar.

CIGARS IN HISTORY:
The Long View

These gentlemen gave us some seegars...
these are leaves of tobacco rolled up in such a manner
that they serve both for a pipe and for tobacco itself.
These the ladies, as well as gentlemen,
are very fond of smoking.

John Cockburn
English traveler in Costa Rica, 1735

I n the wall of an ancient Mayan temple in Palenque, Mexico there is a relief of a man smoking. There could have been a woman, too. All the Mayans smoked tobacco long before 1492, when Christopher Columbus mistook the Caribbean for India, and a member of his crew discovered "Indians" puffing on rolled-up tobacco leaves. They brought the habit home, not exactly what Queen Isabella hoped for when she bankrolled the operation with her country's enrichment in mind. But then nationalism, colonialism, war, and sundry governmental policies have always played a role in the history of the cigar. Like all cultural phenomena, cigars are subject to society's changing mores and the unpredictable swings of economic pendulums, but they have survived for at least two thousand years. The story of the cigar is not over yet.

The Spanish, along with the Portuguese, were the original conquistadors in the New World, and the first Europeans to recognize the beauty of the cigar and to capitalize on its production. Colonialism of the Spanish variety took root in Central and South America, the lands where cigar tobacco grew. (Cuba came under Spanish domination in 1515.) The English missed the cigar boat, so to speak, and so developed first into a pipe-smoking nation with tobacco from Virginia, one of its North American colonies. Evidently, what one smokes depends on what one conquers. It took some time after Columbus' discovery, but by the 1700s the Spanish were growing tobacco in the Western Hemisphere, manufacturing cigars in Spain and exporting them, through Dutch traders, to as far away as Russia.

The smoking room at Nat Sherman Tobacconists.

The Cuban cigar began traveling the world as the map changed. During the eighteenth century, with the battling between European powers, the cigar crossed boundaries and invaded new cultures. In 1763, the British occupied Cuba for a year, more than enough time to fall under the spell of the Cuban cigar. In 1803, when Napoleon invaded Spain, his men discovered Cuban cigars there and galvanized France into begin-

ning its own cigar production.

America got its first taste of the cigar in 1762, when Israel Putnam, an officer in the British army in Cuba, brought the Havana cigar—and a store of Cuban tobacco—back to his home in Connecticut. Tobacco was already being grown in that colony by the settlers, as it was by the Indians before them, but Putnam's contribution inspired the growth of what became one of the world's finest cigar wrappers, Connecticut shade-grown leaf. Putnam later became a general in the American revolution, but he is best remembered for providing the impetus for cigar factories that sprang up in the Hartford, Connecticut area.

Although cigar smoking did not become popular in America until the time of the Civil War, by the late 1800s the United States had developed a sizable cigar industry, which used tobacco grown in several states and imported from Cuba. In the last quarter of the nineteenth century, Cuban immigrants, many fleeing Spanish colonial policies, provided a skilled workforce. Since Florida was their closest point of entry, the state became a mecca with Key West and Tampa producing the greatest proportion of cigars for the country's growing appetite. The Spanish-American War in 1898, which brought a brief Cuban embargo, did not greatly interrupt the momentum.

During this same period, cigars became so well established in Great Britain that the nation was the largest market for Cuban cigars. The aristocracy and the wealthy were devotees. When British financier Leopold de Rothschild requested a particular cigar to fit his lifestyle and taste, one that would have the full flavor of a large ring size, but a body short enough for a brief smoke, the Hoyo de Monterrey factory accommodated him. Thus the world gained the Rothschild, a choice still popular today. Victorian England, renowned for its buttoned-up elegance, perpetuated the cigar's image as an accessory to the life of refinement. Although smoking was frowned upon in public (Queen Victoria disapproved), the after-dinner cigar taken in a separate smoking room, became a beloved indulgence for gentlemen who retired with their colleagues, leaving the scent of exclusivity behind.

In the twentieth century, cigars continued to be buffeted by events far larger than smoking itself. After World War I, the United States industry was nearly crippled by the growing popularity of cigarettes, a less expensive tobacco alternative. But cigar makers fought back with the invention of the cigar-making machine and produced such good quality cheap cigars, still made with all Cuban tobacco, that people could afford them right through the Great Depression. Thus, in the 1930s, worldwide, the cigar, except for handmade Havanas, became everyman's, no longer the preserve of the wealthy and stylish.

World War II and its aftermath brought changes whose reverberations can still be felt today. After the war, cigar prices rose in the United States and companies responded by creating the all-machine-made cigar using homogenized tobacco leaf. This development spawned a huge industry and continued the trend in inexpensive cigars. Havana, alarmed at losing a large segment of the market, also began producing machine-made cigars, which were enormously popular in America—until politics intervened. When Castro came to power, the friction between the United States and its Communist neighbor brought an end to a century-long tobacco relationship.

But as so often happens, when one opportunity is lost, other doors begin to open. As a result of the Cuban nationalization of the cigar industry (into Cubatabaco), and the embargo decreed by President John F. Kennedy in 1962, other countries have stepped into the vacuum. Local talent and Cuban expatriates in the Dominican Republic, Honduras, and Jamaica are now producing excellent cigars with their own distinctive tastes and characters. Mexico, Nicaragua, Ecuador, and Brazil are developing interesting results. The Indonesian islands of Java and Sumatra are contributing fine tobaccos; and excellent wrappers are being grown in Cameroon in Africa. The United States is now a major importer from these sources, and the European nations are obtaining a good portion of their cigars from these countries too.

But the premium cigar and Cuba are still synonymous to connoisseurs, and any curtailment of Havanas caused by natural or political forces seems like a deprivation. The American appetite for Cuban cigars has not so much diminished as gone underground. And the cigar-smoking community, which embraces like-minded people all over the world, eagerly awaits the next political shift, which is bound to change conditions in Cuba and affect the production and availability of the country's cigars. The history of cigars continues to evolve.

HANDMADE CIGARS:
A Listing and Rating

A handmade cigar is like an intricately constructed dessert. It will never be duplicated precisely, and it will not taste exactly the same to everyone. Some will find it sublime; others will agree only that it is very good. Describing a cigar and rating its quality is a similar experience. Taste is a personal matter. The only judgment that can be made is in the consistency of the tobacco blends, the draw, the wrapper, and the construction. The four categories used here are: Superior, Excellent, Very Good and Good. It is important to remember that these assessments are current. Tobacco crops are a living entity with constant fluctuations, and companies change as well. Not every brand appears on the following list, but those that have been selected are the most widely available or are of particular interest. A sampling of the offerings of each company are included.

ARTURO FUENTE

Country Dominican Republic

Flavor Medium to full-bodied taste. The Hemingway Series, with 140 days of extra aging, is mellower.

Quality Superior ◊ ◊ ◊

Distinctions The Fuente family, descendants of the patriarch, Arturo, who made cigars in Cuba at the end of the nineteenth century, are the Dominican Republic's largest producers of handmade cigars. Each year more than five hundred rollers manufacture more than twenty four million cigars. the special character of these cigars stems from the fact that there are over four different types of tobacco in the filler blends.The Fuente family is now pioneering the growth of wrapper leaf in the Dominican Republic, and have already achieved unusual success with the Opus X and Chateau de la Fuente Dominican wrapper.

Canones

Cigar	Category	Length	Ring Size
Canones	Canone	8 $\frac{1}{2}$	52
Chateau Fuente	Robusto	4 $\frac{1}{2}$	50
Churchill	Churchill	7 $\frac{1}{4}$	48
Corona Imperial	Grand Corona	6 $\frac{1}{2}$	46
Curly Head Deluxe	Lonsdale	6 $\frac{1}{2}$	43
Panatela Fina	Long Panatela	7	38
Chateau de la Fuente	Panatela	6	38
Opus X	Robusto	5 $\frac{1}{4}$	50
Hemingway Series			
Short Story	Robusto	4	48
Classic	Churchill	4	48
Masterpiece	Giant	9	52
Signature	Grand Corona	6	47

ASHTON

Country Dominican Republic

Flavor Rich, medium flavor.
   Cabinet Selection: Mild.
   Aged Maduro: Mellow and sweet.

Quality Superior 🍃🍃🍃

Distinctions The elegance of these cigars is a direct result of the style of their originator, William Ashton Taylor, a fine English pipe maker. Their characteristic richness is a result of extra aging, Connecticut wrapper, and Cuban-seed Dominican binder. The Maduro is made with only the darkest of the Connecticut broadleaf wrappers.

8-9-8

Cigar	Category	Length	Ring Size
Churchill	Double Corona	7 1/2	52
Prime Minister	Churchill	6 7/8	48
8-9-8	Lonsdale	6 1/2	44
Panatela	Panatela	6	36
Corona	Corona	5 1/2	44
Cordial	Slim Panatela	5	30
Magnum	Robusto	5	50
Elegante	Panatela	6 1/2	35
Ashton Aged Cabinet Selection			
No. 1	Giant	9	52
No. 2	Churchill	7	46
No. 3	Grand Corona	6	46
Ashton Aged Maduro			
No. 60	Double Corona	7 1/2	52
No. 50	Churchill	7	48
No. 40	Toro	6	50
No. 30	Lonsdale	6 3/4	44
No. 20	Corona	5 1/2	44

Country Dominican Republic

Flavor Medium flavor with a hint of richness.

Quality Superior 🍃🍃🍃

Distinctions Avo is the brand created in 1986 by the renowned musician Avo Uvezian, a Lebanese-born American entrepreneur famous for writing the song "Strangers in the Night." Created by a true cigar aficionado, Avo is committed to a

No. 4

longer aging period and cigars made only with Connecticut Shade wrapper and Cuban seed Dominican binder and filler.

Cigar	Category	Length	Ring Size
No. 1	Lonsdale	6 ¾	42
No. 2	Toro	6	50
No. 3	Double Corona	7 ½	52
No. 4	Long Panatela	7	38
No. 8	Corona	5 ½	40
Pyramid	Pyramid	7	54
Belicoso	Torpedo	6	50
Petit Belicoso	Torpedo	4 ½	50
XO Series			
Maestoso	Churchill	7	48
Preludio	Long Corona	6	40

Country Honduras

Flavor Full-bodied, mild, sweet flavor.

Quality Excellent

Distinctions Owned by a branch of the Upmann family, Baccarat is coming into its own with a blend of Cuban seed, Honduran grown filler, a Mexican binder, and Connecticut shade leaf wrapper. Attractive pricing for a premium cigar makes Baccarat appealing for those with a penchant for sweetness of taste.

Luchadore

Cigar	Category	Length	Ring Size
Bonitas	Small Panatela	4 ½	30
Luchadore	Long Corona	6	43
Polo	Pyramid	7	52
No. 1	Lonsdale	7	44
Churchill	Double Corona	7	50
Rothschild	Robusto	5	50

Country Honduras

Flavor Medium flavor with sweet overtones.

Quality Good ◀

Distinctions Francisco G. Bances, who began this brand in Cuba in 1840, would be surprised to find his name on handmade Honduran cigars as well as machine bunched cigars manufactured in Tampa. When the company moved to Tampa in 1959, with stockpiled Havana leaf, they became the only all-Havana cigar available in the United States after the embargo. Now the handmade Bances is a well-priced Honduran cigar made with local filler and binder tobaccos from Ecuador and Indonesia.

Cigar	Category	Length	Ring Size
Brevas	Corona	5 ½	43
Cazadores	Lonsdale	6 ¼	44
El Prados	Panatela	6 ¼	36
Uniques	Panatela	5 ½	38

Uniques

BAUZA

Country Dominican Republic

Flavor Medium bodied with a rich, aromatic flavor.

Quality Superior

Distinctions Reasonably priced for very good quality, Bauza cigars boast a fine Cameroon wrapper. The filler is Dominican and Nicaraguan, and the binder is Mexican. The Bauza box is reminiscent of the Cuban style before Castro.

Fabulosos

Cigar	Category	Length	Ring Size
Fabulosos	Double Corona	7 ½	50
Casa Grande	Churchill	6 ¾	48
Grecos	Corona	5 ½	42
Jaguar	Lonsdale	6 ½	42
Florete	Panatela	6 ⅞	35
Petit Corona	Short Panatela	5	38

BERING

Country Honduras

Flavor Medium bodied with rich taste and spicy aroma.

Quality Excellent

Distinctions Bering, which began in the Tampa enclave of Ybor City in 1905, is a machine bunched, hand-rolled cigar now made exclusively in Honduras. The brand also produces a range of cigars with maduro and candela wrappers. Bering's brown band indicates its premium cigars, while the red band labels its lower-quality line.

Hispanos

Inmensas

Cigar	Category	Length	Ring Size
Grande	Giant	8 ½	52
Casinos	Lonsdale	7 ⅛	42
Cazadores	Grand Corona	6 ¼	45
Gold No. 1	Slim Panatela	6 ⅛	33
Hispanos	Toro	6	50
Inmensas	Lonsdale	7 ⅛	45
Plazas	Long Corona	6	43

BOLIVAR

Country Cuba

Flavor Full-bodied, rich tasting and aromatic.

Quality Superior

Distinctions The face of Simon Bolivar decorates the band of these cigars, and his picture is a fitting signature—a man of strong character for cigars of equal strength. These are not cigars for the uninitiated, but a smoke for connoisseurs who appreciate their strong flavor, dark wrappers, good draw, and even burn. These are the least expensive of the Havanas and pack plenty of taste for the price. The machine-bunched category is not as strong, and a good choice for beginners. The difference between handmade and machine-bunched should be noted before purchasing.

Belicosos Finos

Cigar	Category	Length	Ring Size
Inmensas	Lonsdale	6 3/4	43
Coronas Gigantes	Churchill	7	47
Palmas	Long Panatela	7	33
Gold Medal Lonsdale	Lonsdale	6 1/2	42
Belicosos Finos	Figuardo	5 1/2	52
Bonitas	Petit Corona	5	40
Royal Coronas	Robusto	4 7/8	50
Bolivar (Machine-made)			
Panatela	Small Panatela	5	35
Champions	Petit Corona	5 1/2	40
Chicos	Cigarillo	4 3/16	29

BUTERA ROYAL
VINTAGE

Country Dominican Republic

Flavor Medium bodied with slightly spicy flavor.

Quality Excellent

Distinctions Pipes are behind the Butera brand, founded in 1993 by pipe carver Mike Butera. The special flavor of these cigars could be found in their binder, which is an aged Java leaf. The filler is Cuban seed Dominican and the wrapper is Connecticut shade leaf. Cedar shavings, sprinkled among the boxed cigars, adds to their flavor.

Cigar	Category	Length	Ring Size
Capo Grande	Churchill	7 1/2	48
Dorado 652	Toro	6	62
Cedro Fino	Lonsdale	6 1/2	44
Bravo Corto	Robusto	4 1/2	50
Cornetta No. 1	Pyramid	6	52
Fumo Dolce	Corona	5 1/2	44
Mira Bella	Panatela	6 3/4	38

CASA BLANCA

Country Dominican Republic

Flavor Extremely mild taste.

Quality Superior 🌿🌿🌿

Distinctions Casa Blanca, "white house" in English, was originally created for use in the White House. These were the cigars lit in celebration of Ronald Reagan's ascendancy to the presidency. Big enough for any festivity, Casa Blanca cigars are famous for their size, the gigantic Jeroboam and half Jeroboam, in particular. But despite their intimidating length and girth, these monsters, made of Dominican and Brazilian filler, Mexican binder, and Connecticut shade wrapper, are very mild.

Presidente

Cigar	Category	Length	Ring Size
Jeroboam	Giant	10	66
Half Jeroboam	Corona Extra	5	66
Magnum	Double Corona	7	60
DeLuxe	Toro	6	50
Presidente	Double Corona	7 1/2	50
Bonitas	Short Panatela	4	36
Panatela	Panatela	6	36

COHIBA

Country Cuba

Flavor Medium bodied, full flavored.

Quality Superior 🍃 🍃 🍃

Distinctions Cohiba, *the* fabled brand of Cuba, was created in 1968 for the express use of the privileged few—the very few—Fidel Castro and the diplomats and heads of state who visited him. Although now widely available, the legends surrounding the brand, its exclusivity, and high price still support its position as the premier cigar in the world. Its reputation is well-deserved. Only the finest tobacco leaves from the most select Cuban *vegas* (farms) are used in Cohibas. The tobacco undergoes an extra, flavor-enhancing period of fermentation. The cigars are rolled only by the most masterful and experienced rollers. And a relatively small number of these cigars are produced, making them all the more sought after. The Linea 1492 series was issued in 1992 to commemorate the five-hundredth anniversary of Columbus' discovery of cigars. Aficionados might consider his discovery of North America as inconsequen-

Cigar	Category	Length	Ring Size
Esplendido	Churchill	7	47
Lanceros	Long Panatela	7 $^9/_{16}$	38
Coronoas Especiales	Panatela	6	38
Robustos	Robusto	4 $^7/_8$	50
Exquisitos	Belvedere	4 $^{15}/_{16}$	36
Cohiba Linea 1492 Range—Siglo Series			
Siglo I	Half Corona	4	40
Siglo II	Petit Corona	5 $^1/_{16}$	42
Siglo III	Lonsdale	6 $^1/_8$	42
Siglo IV	Corona Extra	5 $^5/_8$	46
Siglo V	Grand Corona	6 $^3/_4$	43

tial by comparison. Connoisseurs the world over recognize each other when they hold the distinctive orange, white, and black Cohiba label in hand.

Robustos

Siglo IV

Esplendido

CUBA ALIADOS

Country Honduras

Flavor Medium bodied with a nutty flavor.

Quality Excellent

Distinctions The "General" in this brand, at eighteen inches, is the largest commercially produced cigar in the world. And a very good one. Master blender Rolando Reyes works with Brazilian and Dominican filler, Cuban seed Honduran binder, and Sumatra seed Ecuadorian wrapper to produce these rich-tasting cigars. They are available in Claro, Double Claro, and Colorado shades.

Figurin

Cigar	Category	Length	Ring Size
Piramedes	Pyramid	7 1/2	60
General	Giant	18	66
Palma	Long Panatela	7	36
Lonsdale	Lonsdale	6 1/2	42
Toro	Toro	6	54
Petite Cetro	Short Panatela	5	36
Rothschild	Robusto	5	51
No. 4	Corona Extra	5 1/2	45

Country Dominican Republic

Flavor Mild

Quality Superior

Distinctions The hyphenated Cuesta-Rey name is a legacy of the original nineteenth century founders of this venerable company. The twentieth century incarnation includes machine-made Cuesta-Rays manufactured in Tampa and fine long filler cigars handcrafted in the Dominican Republic. The cigars of the Centennial Collection, which commemorates the founding of the company in 1884, are a combination of Dominican

Cabinet Collection No. 1884

and Brazilian tobaccos aged thirty-five days before boxing. The wrappers are Connecticut and Cameroon and the binders are Dominican.

Cigar	Category	Length	Ring Size
Centennial Collection			
Dominican No. 1	Giant	8 1/2	52
Dominican No. 2	Churchill	7 1/4	48
Dominican No. 3	Long Panatela	7	36
Dominican No. 4	Lonsdale	6 1/2	42
Dominican No. 5	Corona	5 1/2	43
Captiva (aluminum tube)	Long Corona	6 1/8	42
Aristocrat (glass tube)	Churchill	7 1/4	48
Cameo	Small Panatela	4 1/4	32
Cabinet Collection			
No. 1	Giant	8 1/2	52
No. 2	Long Panatela	7	36
No. 95	Lonsdale	6 1/4	42
No. 898	Double Corona	7	49
No. 1884	Lonsdale	6 3/4	44

DAVIDOFF

Country Dominican Republic

Flavor Distinguished by different blends
for various series.
Aniversario Series: very mild.
Grand Cru Series: robust.
Thousand Series: medium flavor.

Quality Superior

Distinctions An appreciation of cigars enhances many peoples' lives. For Zino Davidoff, cigars *were* his life. Born in Russia, Davidoff's fascination with tobacco began as a child in his father's tobacco shop. The family fled to Geneva in 1911, the original site of the Davidoff cigar empire, which now extends to thirty-five countries where elegant emporiums sell men's toiletries and luxurious accessories, in addition to pipes and cigars. Young

Cigar	Category	Length	Ring Size
Aniversario Series			
Aniversario No. 1	Giant	$8\,^2/_3$	48
Aniversario No. 2	Churchill	7	48
Grand Series			
Grand Cru No. 1	Lonsdale	$6\,^1/_8$	42
Grand Cru No. 2	Corona	$5\,^5/_8$	42
Grand Cru No. 3	Petit Corona	5	42
Grand Cru No. 5	Petit Corona	4	40
Special Series			
Double R	Double Corona	$7\,^1/_2$	50
Special r	Robusto	5	50
Special T	Pyramid	6	52
Thousand Series			
1000	Small Panatela	$4\,^5/_8$	34
2000	Petit Corona	5	42
5000	Grand Corona	$5\,^5/_8$	46

Grand Cru No. 5

Grand Cru No. 3

Zino began his romance with cigars in the 1920s when he traveled to Cuba, a connection that eventually developed into an agreement to create his own line of Cuban cigars. This legendary relationship lasted until 1989 and made Davidoff the premier purveyor of cigars in the world. In 1990, Davidoff began producing cigars in the Dominican Republic and even though the blends are, by necessity, different, the quality remains among the best in the world. Zino Davidoff died in 1994 at the age of eighty-eight.

DON DIEGO

Country Dominican Republic

Flavor Mild to medium bodied.

Quality Excellent

Distinctions Don Diego offers cigars in claro and colorado claro wrappers with mild taste and consistent construction. Some sizes are made in both AMS (double claro) and EMS (colorado) wrappers. The filler and binder are Dominican and the wrappers are either Connecticut or Cameroon, which imparts a sweeter taste.

Coronas Bravas

Cigar	Category	Length	Ring Size
Babies	Small Panatela	5	33
Coronas Bravas	Toro	6 1/2	48
Coronas Major (tubed)	Petit Corona	5	42
Grecos	Panatela	6 1/2	38
Imperial	Churchill	7 1/4	46
Lonsdales	Lonsdale	6 5/8	42
Monarchs	Churchill	7 1/4	46

DON TOMAS

Country Honduras

Flavor Full to medium bodied with overtones of coffee and mocha.

Quality Superior

Distinctions The various Don Tomas series have different levels of pricing, the most expensive being the International which is made with an all-Cuban seed blend of tobaccos and is distinguished by a slanting band. The Special Edition features tobaccos grown in Honduras using Connecticut, Cuban, and Dominican seeds.

Cigar	Category	Length	Ring Size
Gigantes	Giant	8 1/2	5 1/2
Presidentes	Double Corona	7 1/2	52
Imperiales No. 1	Giant Corona	8	50
Panatela Largas	Long Panatela	7	44
Toros	Corona Extra	5 1/2	38
Matadors	Corona	5 1/2	46
Rothschild	Robusto	4 1/2	42
			50
Don Tomas International Series			
No. 1	Lonsdale	6 1/2	
No. 2	Robusto	5 1/2	44
No. 3	Corona	5 1/2	50
			42
Don Tomas Special Edition			
No. 100	Double Corona	7 1/2	
No. 200	Lonsdale	6 1/2	50
No. 500	Corona Extra		44

Don Tomas No. 2

DUNHILL

Country Dominican Republic

Flavor Medium bodied and medium flavored.

Quality Superior 🍃🍃🍃

Distinctions Since 1989, when Dunhill began manufacturing in the Dominican Republic, the company has concentrated on its "Aged Cigars," vintage cigars with all the tobacco taken from one year. The year of the vintage is printed on the box, and every cigar is aged in cedar for at least three months. The vintage blends feature Piloto Cubano and Olor tobaccos from the renowned Cibao Valley in the Dominican Republic. The wrappers are Connecticut shade-grown leaf. Handsomely adorned with the blue-and-white Dunhill band, they are very successfully sold worldwide. Dunhill cigars with a black-and-white band, made in the Canary Islands, are a good handmade product with a mild flavor, but not of the Dominican caliber. In addition, there are small "dry" Dunhills manufactured in Holland.

Cigar	Category	Length	Ring Size
Centenas	Torpedo	6	50
Cabreras (tubed)	Churchill	7	48
Peravias	Churchill	7	50
Romanas	Rothschild	4 ½	50
Fantinos	Panatela	7	28
Valverdes	Corona	5 ½	42
Diamantes	Lonsdale	6 ⅝	42
Samanas	Panatela	6 ½	38

Cigar	Category	Length	Ring Size
Dunhill (Canary Islands)			
Panatelas	Slim Panatela	6	30
Lonsdale Grandes	Lonsdale	7 ½	42
Coronas	Corona	5 ½	43

Centenas

EL REY DEL MUNDO

Country Cuba

Flavor Mild bodied with a subtle aroma.

Quality Superior 🌿🌿🌿

Distinctions El Rey del Mundo means "King of the World," a brave declaration of quality that is not without some justification. This brand was established in 1848 and produces a large selection. Their light flavor makes these cigars most suitable for daytime smoking, and a good introduction to the Cuban cigar.

Lunch Club

Gran Corona

Cigar	Category	Length	Ring Size
Tainos	Churchill	7	47
Choix Supreme	Robusto	5	48
Lonsdale	Lonsdale	6 $1/2$	42
Grandes de Espana	Long Panatela	7 $9/16$	38
Elegantes	Slim Panatela	6 $7/8$	28
Petit Coronas	Petit Corona	5 $1/16$	42
Coronas de Luxe	Corona	5 $9/16$	42
Lunch Club	Tres Petit Corona	4	42
Gran Corona	Grand Corona	5 $1/2$	46

EL REY DEL MUNDO

Country Honduras

Flavor Full, heavy bodied flavor.

Quality Superior

Distinctions Cigars produced in Honduras with the El Rey del Mundo name are much heavier in flavor than those with the Cuban brand. There are forty-seven varieties in a large number of shapes, some of which are tubed. Their strong flavor stems from a Honduran blended filler and binder, and a Sumatran seed Ecuadorian wrapper. There are a number of lighter cigars made by this company, which feature filler tobacco from the Dominican Republic, a Honduran binder and a Connecticut wrapper.

Cigar	Category	Length	Ring Size
Robusto Zavalla	Robusto	5	54
Tino	Panatela	$5\,1/2$	38
Rectangulares	Grand Corona	$5\,5/8$	45
Flor de Llaneza	Torpedo	$6\,1/2$	54
Principale	Churchill	8	47
Cedars	Londsdale	7	43
Lighter Series with Dominican tobacco filler			
Robusto Zavalla	Robusto	5	54

Flor de Llaneza

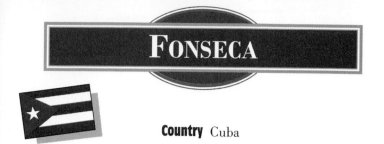

FONSECA

Country Cuba

Flavor Medium body with light flavor.

Quality Very Good

Distinctions Cuba's Fonseca is an unusual brand that makes only five cigars, four of which are handmade. Ideal for beginners, the cigars have a lightness and softness. The No. 1 may be the lightest of all the Cuban Lonsdales, a cigar with good balance of strength and flavor. Their most unusual characteristic is the white tissue paper in which they are wrapped, which affords them an image in keeping with their gentle flavor. These cigars are only widely available in Spain and Switzerland.

Cigar	Category	Length	Ring Size
Invictos	Figurado	5 $\frac{1}{4}$	45
Fonseca No. 1	Lonsdale	6 $\frac{3}{8}$	44
Cosacos	Corona	5 $\frac{1}{2}$	42
K.D.T. Cadetes	Demi-Tasse	4 $\frac{9}{16}$	36

Cosacos

FONSECA

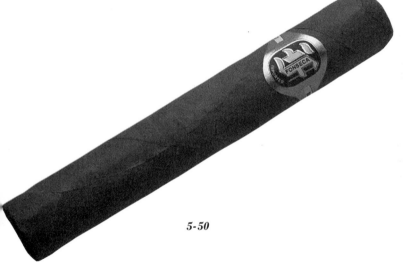

Country Dominican Republic

Flavor Medium bodied with mild flavor.

Quality Excellent 🍃🍃

Distinctions The Dominican Fonseca brand cigars are made with specially grown Dominican filler, a Mexican binder, and a choice of Connecticut wrapper, natural or maduro. The pyramid is unusually well-constructed with a rich flavor.

5-50

Cigar	Category	Length	Ring Size
8-9-8	Long Corona	6	43
7-9-9	Grand Corona	6 1/2	46
5-50	Robusto	5	50
2-2	Petit Corona	4 1/4	40
Triangular	Pyramid	5 1/2	56

GRIFFIN'S

Country Dominican Republic

Flavor Medium bodied with spicy flavor.

Quality Superior

Distinctions Griffin's cigars are an elegant brand with a price to match. These are high-quality cigars with a filler made of three different superior Dominican tobaccos. The binder is also Dominican and the wrapper Connecticut. Their mildness makes them especially good for a daytime smoke. The cigars are distributed exclusively by Davidoff, the result of an association in Geneva with Zino Davidoff that began many years ago.

No. 400

Cigar	Category	Length	Ring Size
Prestige	Giant	7 1/2	50
Privilege	Slim Panatela	5	32
No. 100	Long Panatela	7	38
No. 200	Lonsdale	7	43
No. 300	Long Corona	6 1/4	43
No. 400	Panatela	6	38

H. UPMANN

Country Cuba

Flavor Medium body with smooth flavor.

Quality Superior 🍃 🍃 🍃

Distinctions The H. in Upmann is for Herman, a European banker who transformed his passion for cigars into a factory in Cuba in 1844. The family worked in banking and cigars successfully for only forty years, but the brand continues to be well-respected, indeed legendary, to this day. Its factory is one of the oldest continuous cigar manufacturing sites in Cuba. Smokers should be forewarned that H. Upmann produces a bewildering number of

Corona Amatista

Sir Winston Churchill

cigars, many of which are machine-made of a quality that does not come close to the handmade. (Beware—their machine-made are even sold in tubes.) Only handmade Upmanns are imported into Great Britain.

Cigar	Category	Length	Ring Size
Magnum	Corona Extra	5 3/4	43
Sir Winston	Churchill	7	47
Super Corona	Grand Corona	5 1/2	46
Culebras	Culebras	5 3/4	39
Cristales	Corona	5 5/16	42
Connoisseur No. 1	Robusto	5 7/16	48
Cinco Bocas	Lonsdale	6 1/2	42
Kings	Petit Corona	5 1/16	42
Amatista	Corona	5 3/4	40
Seleccion Suprema	Long Panatela	7	33
Upmann No. 1	Lonsdale	6 1/2	42
Upmann No. 2	Pyramid	6 1/8	52

H. UPMANN

Country Dominican Republic

Flavor Mild to medium flavor with sweet overtones.

Quality Superior 🍃 🍃 🍃

Distinctions The Dominican H. Upmann is a cigar of dependable consistency and a hint of sweetness. An Indonesian wrapper has recently replaced the traditional Cameroon, but the binder and filler remain Cuban seed Dominican grown. This company produces an especially good selection of tubed, humidified cigars. "H. Upmann, 1844" appears on the label of the Dominican Upmanns in contrast the Havanas, which are marked "H. Upmann Habana."

Lonsdales

Cigar	Category	Length	Ring Size
Lonsdales	Lonsdale	6 ⅝	42
Amatista	Long Corona	5 ⅞	42
Churchills	Grand Corona	5 ⅝	46
Corona Imperiales	Churchill	7	46
Emperadores	Churchill	7 ¾	46
Extra Finose Gold (tubed)	Panatela	6 ¾	38

HENRY CLAY

Country Dominican Republic

Flavor Medium to full bodied.

Quality Very Good

Distinctions In the first quarter of the nineteenth century, Henry Clay was a United States congressman, speaker of the house, senator, and secretary of state. The cigars that bear his name are not nearly as prodigious—there are only three. Originally made in Cuba, they are now a Dominican cigar with filler and binder of that island and an excellent mid-brown Connecticut broadleaf wrapper. The Cuban factory, which began when Clay was a politician, is still pictured on the labels of the boxes. Different blends are sold in Europe than in the United States.

Cigar	Category	Length	Ring Size
Brevas	Corona	5 ½	42
Brevas a la Conserva	Corona Extra	5 ⅝	46
Brevas Finas	Churchill	6 ½	48

Brevas Finas

HOYO DE MONTERREY

Country Cuba

Flavor Medium bodied and mild.
Le Hoyo series is more full-flavored.

Quality Superior 🍃🍃🍃

Distinctions A "hoyo" is a dip in the land or a valley, and the Hoyo de Monterrey is a sweet spot within the supreme tobacco-growing territory of the Vuelta Abajo's Pinar del Rio region of Cuba. The company named for this valley was founded in 1867 and is one of Cuba's oldest. Today the brand, which was one of the first ever created in Cuba, produces cigars that are quite a bit milder. The Le Hoyo range, a sub-brand, is more full-bodied.

Le Hoyo du Auphin

Cigar	Category	Length	Ring Size
Particulares	Giant	9 1/2	47
Churchill	Churchill	7	47
Concorde	Churchill	7	47
Super Selection No. 1	Lonsdale	6 1/8	42
Opera	Corona	5 9/16	42
Odeon	Panatela	5 5/16	38
Versailles	Slim Panatela	6 3/4	33
Jeanne D'Arc	Panatela	5 5/8	35
Le Hoyo du Roi	Corona	5 9/16	42
Le Hoyo du Prince	Petit Corona	5 1/8	42
Le Hoyo du Auphin	Corona Especial	7	38

HOYO DE MONTERREY

Country Honduras

Flavor Medium to heavy bodied with strong, full flavor.

Quality Superior

Distinctions A much more full-flavored cigar than the Cuban of this name, the Honduran Hoyo de Monterrey has a Nicaraguan, Honduran, and Cuban seed Dominican blended filler, a Connecticut binder and an Ecuadorian-grown Sumatra wrapper. The combination, more than a sum of its parts, results in a very full-flavored cigar. The Honduran band is maroon as opposed to the Cuban red. There is an additional series with quite a different flavor that is sold in the United States as Hoyo de Monterrey Excalibur, but is known simply as Excalibur in Europe.

Cigar	Category	Length	Ring Size
President	Giant	8 1/2	52
Sultan	Double Corona	7 1/4	54
Governor	Toro	8 1/8	50
Café Royale (tubed)	Corona	5 5/8	43
Churchill	Grand Corona	6 1/4	45
Cuban Largos	Churchill	7 1/4	47
Dreams	Grand Corona	5 3/4	46
Super Hoyos	Corona	5 1/2	44
Culebras	Culebras	6	35
No. 55	Corona	5 1/4	43
Delights	Panatela	6 1/4	47

J. R. ULTIMATE

Country Honduras

Flavor Full-bodied with Havana style flavor.

Quality Superior 🍃 🍃 🍃

Distinctions The J.R. Tobacco Company of America, a testament to the entrepreneurial skills of founder Lew Rothman, is a mail order, wholesale, and retail operation that handles a large percentage of all premium cigars sold in the United States. The company's *raison d'etre* is excellent prices, but it also produces some fine cigars of its own. J.R. Ultimates, made with Cuban seed tobaccos from Honduras and wrappers in multiple shades, have the advantage of being aged for one year. The company, which also manufactures cigars in the Dominican Republic, produces two additional series there, Special Coronas and Special Jamaicans, both milder in flavor than the J.R. Ultimates.

Corona

Cigar	Category	Length	Ring Size
Cetro	Lonsdale	7	42
Corona Tubos (tubed)	Grand Corona	5 5/8	45
Estelo Individual	Giant	6 3/4	58
No. 1	Double Corona	7 1/4	54
No. 5	Long Corona	6 1/8	44
Padron	Toro	6	54
Rothschild	Robusto	4 1/2	50
Super Cetro	Giant Corona	8 1/4	43

JOYA DE NICARAGUA

Country Nicaragua

Flavor Medium bodied with a peppery flavor.

Quality Very Good

Distinctions Because of superior tobacco-growing soil, Nicaraguan cigars were once considered the closest to Havanas in the world, but in recent history, war and politics have played havoc with this brand. Now cigars from the company called "Jewel of Nicaragua" are improving as stability in the country increases. The filler and binder are of Cuban seed Nicaraguan grown tobaccos, and the wrapper is Connecticut leaf. As the tobacco fields recover, this company, founded by Cuban expatriates, is expected to produce excellent cigars.

Viajante

Cigar	Category	Length	Ring Size
Presidente	Double Corona	7 1/2	50
No. 1	Lonsdale	6 5/8	44
No. 5	Panatela	6 7/8	35
No. 6	Toro	6	52
Viajante	Giant	8 1/2	52

JUAN CLEMENTE

Country Dominican Republic

Flavor Medium bodied with complex flavor. Club Selection is more robust.

Quality Superior

Distinctions 1982 is the year Frenchman Jean Clement began producing cigars in the Dominican Republic and gave them his name, Spanish style, Juan Clemente. The unusual manufacturing program of the company makes the cigars both excellent and hard to find. Clement chose not to organize his business in conjunction with a tax-reduced government program that encourages exporting. Thus the company, which only produces about 450,000 cigars a year, can sell to tourists, which leaves fewer cigars for the rest of the world. Because of its size, the concern can buy some outstanding tobaccos that are only available in quantities too small for larger companies. In addition, the filler blend is made up of four different tobaccos, offering an interesting, complex taste. The binder in Juan Clemente cigars is Dominican and the wrapper Connecticut shade leaf. To distinguish these cigars further, they do not have a traditional band, but a silver-paper wrapping over the foot with a band holding it in place.

Panatela

Cigar	Category	Length	Ring Size
Grand Corona	Long Corona	6	42
Panatela	Panatela	6 ½	34
Especiale	Long Panatela	7 ½	38
530	Small Panatela	5	30
Gargantua	Giant	13	50
Club Selection No. 3	Lonsdale	7	44

JUAN LOPEZ

Country Cuba

Flavor Mild

Quality Excellent

Distinctions Limited to only six models, Juan Lopez is a very small and very old Cuban company. The cigars are unusually light for Havanas and are most suitable for daytime smoking.

Cigar	Category	Length	Ring Size
Corona	Corona	$5\,5/8$	42
Slimaranas	Small Panatela	$4\,15/16$	34
Petit Corona	Petit Corona	$5\,1/8$	42
Patricias	Half Corona	$4\,5/8$	40
Selection No. 2	Robusto	$4\,7/8$	50

Petit Corona

LA CORONA VINTAGE

Country Dominican Republic

Flavor Mild to medium flavored.

Quality Excellent 🍃 🍃

Distinctions La Corona is an old Cuban name, but without a continuting legacy in that country. Today fine La Corona cigars are produced in the Dominican Republic with Dominican filler and binder and Connecticut wrapper. However, there are still some La Corona cigars made in Cuba, but they are machine-made and should be carefully distinguished from the Dominican hand-made vintage models.

Cigar	Category	Length	Ring Size
Directors	Grand Corona	6 $^1/_2$	46
Aristocrats	Panatela	6 $^1/_{16}$	38
Chicas	Corona	5 $^1/_2$	42
Coronas	Long Corona	6	43

LA FLOR DE CANO

Country Cuba

Flavor Mild with a touch of sweetness.

Quality Superior

Distinctions La Flor de Cano produces nine models, five handmade and four machine-made, so careful notice should be taken of the difference. The Short Churchill is especially noteworthy.

Predilectos Tubulares

Cigar	Category	Length	Ring Size
Diademas	Churchill	7	47
Gran Coronas	Corona Extra	$5\,^5/_8$	47
Selectos	Corona	$5\,^7/_8$	41
Short Churchill	Robusto	$4\,^7/_8$	50
Predilectos Tubulares	Petit Corona	5	42

LA GLORIA CUBANA

Country Cuba

Flavor Medium bodied with a spicy, mellow taste.

Quality Superior 🍂 🍂 🍂

Distinctions La Gloria Cubana is a venerable Cuban name (with a famous yellow band) that was resurrected about twenty years ago and now produces cigars that are accessible to smokers of all levels of experience. Many are good daytime smokes. The Medaille d'Or model, which is manufactured in small quantities, is sold in attractive 8-9-8 varnished boxes.

Cigar	Category	Length	Ring Size
Tainos	Churchill	7	47
Cetros	Lonsdale	6 ½	42
Sabrosos	Lonsdale	6 ⅛	42
Tapados	Corona	5 5/16	42
Minutos	Half Corona	4 9/16	40
Medaille d'Or No. 4	Slim Panatela	6 ⅞	32

Medaille d'Or No. 4

LA GLORIA CUBANA

Country United States

Flavor Full-bodied with excellent balance of strength and flavor.

Quality Superior 🍂🍂🍂

Distinctions Cuban-born Ernesto Crarillo is credited with making the American La Gloria Cubana label an extraordinary cigar. Many believe that these cigars are the closest in the world to Havanas in flavor, texture, and quality. The cigars are made with a filler blend of Dominican, Brazilian, and American tobaccos, a Nicaraguan binder and Ecuador-grown Sumatra wrapper. Those available in maduro are wrapped in Connecticut broad leaf.

Medaille d'Or No. 3

Cigar	Category	Length	Ring Size
Soberano	Giant	8	52
Charlemagne	Double Corona	7 $\frac{1}{4}$	54
Glorias Inmensas	Churchill	7 $\frac{1}{2}$	48
Minutos	Small Panatela	4 $\frac{1}{2}$	40
Medaille d'Or No. 3	Cigarillo	7	28

MACANUDO

Country Jamaica

Flavor Mild and smooth.

Quality Superior 🍃🍃🍃

Distinctions *Macanudo* means "the greatest" in Spanish, and many smokers believe these cigars deserve the compliment. The largest-selling brand in the United States, the name has a long history of association with Cuba, Jamaica, and Great Britain. Today, Macanudos are produced both in Jamaica, and the Dominican Republic, but due to their exceptional consistency, and the exactness of the blend, it is impossible to tell any individual cigar's country of origin. All use Jamaican, Dominican, and Mexican filler, Mexican binder and Connecticut shade wrapper, and an especially long aging process during production adds to their flavor. The brand offers a variety of wrappers: Greenish-brown jade (candela), with a mild flavor; light brown café, with a medium taste; and rich brown maduro from a Mexican leaf. The Vintage Collection is fuller bodied and more costly in what is, in total, a higher-priced brand.

Cigar	Category	Length	Ring Size
Ascot	Small Panatela	4 $\frac{1}{8}$	32
Caviar	Short Panatela	4	36
Claybourne	Slim Panatela	6	31
Lord Claridge	Panatela	5 $\frac{1}{2}$	38
Duke of Devon	Corona	5 $\frac{1}{2}$	42
Portofino (tubed)	Long Panatela	7	42
Hampton Court (tubed)	Corona	5 $\frac{3}{4}$	43
Hyde Park	Robusto	5 $\frac{1}{2}$	49
Baron de Rothschild	Lonsdale	6 $\frac{1}{2}$	42
Pyramid	Torpedo	6 $\frac{1}{2}$	52
Crystal (tubed)	Robusto	5 $\frac{1}{2}$	50
Duke of Wellington	Long Panatela	8 $\frac{1}{2}$	38
Trump	Grand Corona	6 $\frac{1}{2}$	45

Hyde
Park

Hampton
Court

Crystal

Duke of Wellington

Cigar	Category	Length	Ring Size
Vintage Cabinet Selection			
I	Double Corona	7 $\frac{1}{2}$	49
II	Lonsdale	6 $\frac{1}{2}$	43
VII (tubed)	Robusto	5 $\frac{1}{2}$	50
Pyramid	Pyramid	6 $\frac{1}{2}$	52

MONTECRISTO

Country Cuba

Flavor Medium to full-bodied with tangy, aromatic flavor.

Quality Superior 🍃 🍃 🍃

Distinctions Montecristo, a Cuban brand founded in the 1930s, was considered the country's premium until Cohiba was created in 1968. Today, Monetcristo still outsells all other Cubans, with sales of over thirty-million cigars. The brand accounts for the largest percentage of Havanas sold in Spain, a large portion of the French market, and a goodly number in Britain and Switzerland. Recognized by their colorado claro slightly oily wrappers, Montecristos have a unique, tangy flavor. Their box is nearly as famous as their taste. The handsome design of crossed swords and fleur de lys is a reference to *The Count of Montecristo*, the Alexander Dumas novel from which the name is taken.

Montecristo No. 2

Montecristo No. 3

Cigar	Category	Length	Ring Size
A	Grand Corona	9 1/2	47
Tubos	Lonsdale	6 1/8	42
Especial No. 1	Long Panatela	7 9/16	38
Montecristo No. 1	Lonsdale	6 1/2	42
Montecristo No. 2	Panatela	6	38
Montecristo No. 3	Corona	5 9/16	42
Montecristo No. 4	Petit Corona	5 1/16	42
Montecristo No. 5	Half Corona	4	42
Joyitas	Demi-tasse	5 7/8	26

MONTECRUZ

Country Dominican Republic

Flavor Medium to full-bodied.

Quality Superior 🍃 🍃 🍃

Distinctions Montecruz, like many premium brands, is the result of cigar makers fleeing Cuba to carry on elsewhere. In this case the Menendez family, founders of Montecristo, emigrated to the Canary Islands and created a brand with design, taste, and quality similar to their original endeavor. Today Montecruz is produced in the Dominican Republic and recognized especially for its "Sun Grown" line of cigars with Cameroon wrappers. The filler combines Dominican grown Piloto Cubano and Olor with Brazilian tobaccos and the binder is Dominican. In addition to the sun-grown Cameroon, there is a natural claro Connecticut shade wrapper. The blend of the filler is adjusted to complement the taste of the two different wrappers with the Connecticut being the lighter.

No. 201

Cigar	Category	Length	Ring Size
No. 200	Churchill	7 $\frac{1}{4}$	46
No. 201	Grand Corona	6 $\frac{1}{4}$	46
No. 210	Lonsdale	6 $\frac{1}{2}$	42
No. 220	Corona	5 $\frac{1}{2}$	42
No. 250	Panatela	6 $\frac{1}{2}$	38
No. 280	Cigarillo	7	28
A	Lonsdale	6 $\frac{1}{2}$	43
F	Churchill	7 $\frac{1}{4}$	47
Cedar Aged	Petit Corona	5	42
Tubulares (tubed)	Panatela	6 $\frac{1}{8}$	36

NAT SHERMAN

Country Dominican Republic

Flavor **Exchange Selection:** Mild and smooth, Connecticut wrapper.

Landmark Selection: Medium to full bodied, Cameroon wrapper.

Manhattan Selection: Medium bodied, nutlike flavor, Mexican wrapper.

Gotham Selection: Mild, well-balanced, Connecticut wrapper.

City Desk Selection: Full-flavored, maduro wrapper. Medium to full-bodied taste.

V.I.P. Selection: Very mild, smooth, Connecticut wrapper.

Host Selection: Sweet flavor, mild to medium body, cured Connecticut wrapper.

Metropolitan Selection: Full body, distinct bouquet and presence.

Quality Superior

Distinctions The Nat Sherman tobacco emporium at 500 Fifth Avenue in New York sits on a corner with a handsome clock crowning the building. This symbol appears on the bands of Nat Sherman cigars, with different background colors for different series. The com-

Cigar	Category	Length	Ring Size
Exchange Selection			
Academy No. 2	Small Panatela	5	31
Murray Hill No. 7	Panatela	6	38
Butterfield No. 8	Lonsdale	6 1/2	42
Trafalgar No. 4	Grand Corona	6	47
Landmark Selection			
Metropole	Panatela	6	34
Hampshire	Corona	5 1/2	42
Algonquin	Lonsdale	6 3/4	43
Vanderbilt	Grand Corona	6	47

pany offers several, each with a different blend and each named after some element of New York or Sherman family history. The Exchange Selection, for example, features famous phone exchanges of the 1940s. The Landmark and Manhattan categories are named for New York real estate. The City Desk group recognizes legendary newspaper editors. The Gotham Selection commemorates addresses in Sherman lore.

Host Selection: Hobart

Exchange Selection:
Butterfield No. 8

Metropolitan Selection: Anglers

V.I.P. Selection:
Zigfeld "Fancytail"

City Desk
Selection:
Telegraph

Manhattan
Selection:
Gramercy

Landmark
Selection:
Vanderbilt

Gotham
Selection:
1400

Cigar	Category	Length	Ring Size
Manhattan Selection			
Beekman	Cigarillo	5 1/4	28
Tribeca	Slim Panatela	6	31
Gramercy	Lonsdale	6 3/4	43
Sutton	Robusto	5 1/2	49
Chelsea	Panatela	6 1/2	38
Gotham Selection			
No. 65	Slim Panatela	6	32
No. 1400	Long Corona	6 1/4	44
No. 711	Toro	6	50
No. 500	Double Corona	7	50
City Desk Selection			
Gazette	Long Corona	6	42
Dispatch	Grand Corona	6 1/2	46
Telegraph	Toro	6	50
Tribune	Double Corona	7 1/2	50
V.I.P. Selection			
Zigfeld "Fancytail"	Perfecto	6 3/4	38
Morgan	Lonsdale	7	42
Astor	Rothchild	4 1/2	50
Carnegie	Toro	6	48
Host Selection			
Hudson	Small Panetatela	6	34
Hamilton	Corona	5 1/2	42
Hunter	Long Corona	6 3/4	43
Harrington	Lonsdale	7 1/2	47
Hobart	Robust	5 1/2	49
Hampton	Double Corona	7	50
Metropolitan Selection			
Anglers	Corona	5 1/2	43
Nautical	Trumpet	7	34/48
University	Toro	6	50
Explorers	Petit Piramide	5 1/2	44/56
Metropolitan	Piramide	7	47/60

ONYX

Country Dominican Republic

Flavor Mild.

Quality Very Good

Distinctions This brand was launched in 1992, and is of interest as a specialty in Mexican maduro wrappers. The cigars have a Java binder and a filler of Dominican grown Piloto Cubano, Olor, and Mexican tobaccos.

No. 650

Cigar	Category	Length	Ring Size
No. 642	Long Corona	6	42
No. 646	Grand Corona	6 ⅝	46
No. 650	Toro	5	50
No. 852	Giant	8	52

OSCAR

Country Dominican Republic

Flavor Medium-bodied.

Quality Excellent 🍃🍃

Distinctions There are only six Oscars, but the small group covers a range for most smoking opportunities. The large 9 x 46 Don Oscar is balanced by the Oscarito, which is pleasantly full-bodied for a small cigar. The filler and binder are excellently grown Dominican tobaccos and the wrapper is Connecticut shade leaf. A line of more full-bodied cigars is produced for the European market.

No. 600

Cigar	Category	Length	Ring Size
Don Oscar	Giant	9	46
No. 200	Lonsdale	7	44
No. 300	Long Corona	6 $\frac{1}{4}$	44
No. 500	Robusto	5 $\frac{1}{2}$	50
No. 600	Robusto	4 $\frac{1}{2}$	50
No. 700	Pyramid	7	54
Oscarito	Cigarillo	4	20
Prince	Short Panatela	5	30

PARTAGAS

Country Cuba

Flavor Full bodied, with an earthy flavor.

Quality Superior 🍃🍃🍃

Distinctions Partagas is one of the oldest names in cigars, founded in the 1840s by Don Jaime Partagas. Today the company produces fifty-eight models—twenty-eight handmade, thirty machine-made and twenty-five machine-bunched and hand finished. The handmade are outstanding, but the rest are not necessarily, so purchasing demands an awareness of the process. After 150 years, the cigars are still made in the same nineteenth century factory in downtown Havana.

Serie du Connaisseur No. 4   Partagas de Partagas No. 1   8-9-8   Lusitania

Cigar	Category	Length	Ring Size
Lusitania	Double Corona	7 5/8	49
Churchill Deluxe	Churchill	7	47
Presidente	Grand Corona	6 1/8	47
Partagas de Partagas No. 1	Grand Corona	6 3/4	43
Partagas 8-9-8	Lonsdale	6 1/8	42
Serie du Connaisseur No. 1	Long Panatela	7 9/16	36
Coronas "A" Mejorado	Corona	5 9/16	42
Serie du Connaisseur No. 4	Robusto	4 7/8	50
Tres Petit Coronas	Half Corona	4 9/16	40
Lonsdale	Lonsdale	6 1/2	42

PARTAGAS

Country Dominican Republic

Flavor Medium to full bodied, rich tasting with a touch of sweetness.

Quality Superior

Distinctions The full flavor of these cigars is a result of the Dominican, Jamaican, and Mexican tobaccos in the filler, the Mexican binder, and the Cameroon wrapper. In celebration of the 150th anniversary of the brand, there is limited edition Signature Series made with aged Cameroon wrappers sold in boxes of twenty-five, fifty, and one hundred. The Cuban version of Partagas has "Habana" on the band, while the Dominican is marked with "Partagas 1845."

Cigar	Category	Length	Ring Size
Puritos	Small Panatela	4 $\frac{1}{8}$	32
No. 3	Corona	5 $\frac{1}{4}$	43
Robusto	Robusto	4 $\frac{1}{2}$	49
No. 2	Corona	5 $\frac{3}{4}$	43
No. 1	Lonsdale	6 $\frac{3}{4}$	43
Sabroso (tubed)	Long Corona	5 $\frac{7}{8}$	44
Tubos (tubed)	Slim Panatela	7	34
Almirnates	Grand Corona	6 $\frac{1}{4}$	47
8-9-8	Lonsdale	6 $\frac{7}{8}$	44
Limited Reserve Royale	Lonsdale	6 $\frac{3}{4}$	43
Limited Reserve Regale	Grand Corona	6 $\frac{1}{4}$	47

8-9-8

Almirnates

PAUL GARMIRIAN

Country Dominican Republic

Flavor Medium to full bodied with a pleasant spiciness.

Quality Superior 🍃 🍃 🍃

Distinctions Paul Garmirian's P.G. cigars are the work of a true aficionado who gave full reign to his passion and started his own company. That was in 1991, and the cigars, produced in limited quantities, are widely admired. Comparable in many ways to fine Havanas, the P.G. features a dark reddish-brown colorado colored Connecticut shade leaf wrapper with Dominican binder and filler. Garmirian is the author of *The Gourmet Guide to Cigars.*

Petit Bouquet

Cigar	Category	Length	Ring Size
P.G. Celebration	Giant	9	50
P.G. Belicoso	Torpedo	6 $^1/_4$	52
P.G. Churchill	Churchill	7	48
P.G. No. 1	Long Panatela	7 $^1/_2$	38
P.G. Corona Grande	Grand Corona	6 $^1/_2$	46
P.G. Lonsdale	Lonsdale	6 $^1/_2$	42
P.G. Connoisseur	Toro	6	50
P.G. Epicure	Robusto	5 $^1/_2$	50
P.G. Corona	Corona	5 $^1/_2$	42
P.G. Petit Bouquet	Short Panatela	4 $^1/_2$	38

PLEIADES

Country Dominican Republic

Flavor Mild to medium bodied.

Quality Very Good

Distinctions These cigars with a celestial name have dual nationalities, Dominican and French. They are made in the Dominican Republic with Olor and Piloto Cubano filler, Dominican binder and Connecticut shade leaf wrapper. The cigars then travel the Atlantic to the company's home in France, where they age for six months and undergo careful sorting and packing. An interesting side note is the Pleiades box, which is made in the Netherlands and has a built-in, rechargeable Credo humidifer.

Sirius

Cigar	Category	Length	Ring Size
Aldebaran	Giant	8 1/2	50
Neptune	Giant Corona	7 1/2	42
Sirius	Churchill	6 7/8	46
Centaurus	Corona	5 3/4	42
Uranus	Panatela	6 7/8	34
Pluton	Robusto	5	50
Perseus	Small Panatela	5	34
Venus	Cigarillo	5 1/2	28

POR LARRANAGA

Country Cuba

Flavor Medium to full bodied with a touch of sweetness.

Quality Superior 🍃🍃🍃

Distinctions A venerable Cuban brand, the oldest still in operation, Por Larranaga cigars are not widely distributed, but are sought after by connoisseurs of true Havanas. The company, which was the first to introduce mechanization to cigar making, produces machine-made and handmade cigars in the same sizes. Larranaga is named in Rudyard Kipling's famous poem in which he wrote, "A woman is only a woman, but a good cigar is a smoke." Unfortunately.

Cigar	Category	Length	Ring Size
Lonsdale	Lonsdale	$6\,1/2$	42
Lancero	Corona	$5\,9/16$	42
Petit Corona	Petit Corona	$5\,1/16$	42
Nectares No. 4	Corona Extra	$4\,9/16$	40
Coronita	Panatela	5	38

Coronita

POR LARRANAGA

Country Dominican Republic

Flavor Medium to full bodied.

Quality Superior 🍃🍃🍃

Distinctions Por Larranagas of the Dominican Republic
are excellently made, with fillers of Dominican and
Brazilian tobaccos, Dominican binders, and
Connecticut shade leaf wrappers. The selection is
small, only seven sizes, and not widely available. The
word "Habana" appears on the bands of the Cuban
brand, and on the Dominican, "La Romana."

Pyramid

Cigar	Category	Length	Ring Size
Fabulosos	Double Corona	7	50
Cetros	Lonsdale	6 $\frac{7}{8}$	42
Nacionales	Corona	5 $\frac{1}{2}$	42
Delicados	Panatela	6 $\frac{1}{2}$	36
Pyramid	Perfecto	6	48

PUNCH

Country Cuba

Flavor Mild to medium bodied with a tangy flavor.

Quality Superior 🍃🍃🍃

Distinctions This brand was created in 1840 for the British market, and was named for the humor magazine *Punch,* whose insignia was a character called Mr. Punch sporting a cigar. His image still decorates the brand's boxes. Today Punch is popular worldwide, and popularly priced, a fact that perversely makes the brand less appealing to connoisseurs. There are a large number of models, including many that are machine-made in the same sizes as those that are handmade, so caution should be taken. Also, the same-sized cigars may have different names in different countries.

Cigar	Category	Length	Ring Size
Diademas	Grand Corona	9 $1/_2$	47
Double Coronas	Double Corona	7 $5/_8$	49
Monarcas	Churchill	7	47
Punch Punch	Corona Extra	5 $5/_8$	46
Black Prince	Corona Extra	5 $5/_8$	46
Seleccion de Luxe No. 1	Corona Extra	5 $5/_8$	46
Nectares No. 5	Long Panatela	7	33
Super Selection No. 1	Lonsdale	6 $1/_8$	42
Presidentes	Petit Corona	5 $1/_{16}$	42
Petit Punch de Luxe	Half Corona	4	40

Punch Punch

PUNCH

Country Honduras

Flavor Full bodied.

Quality Superior

Distinctions The Punch brand of Honduras is one of the best of that country, with the full flavor characteristic of the island's cigar industry. The cigars' filler is of Honduran, Dominican, and Nicaraguan tobacco, with a Connecticut binder and an Ecuadorian-grown Sumatra wrapper. The robust flavor of the Grand Cru Series is a result of tobacco that has been aged three to five years.

Britania

Cigar	Category	Length	Ring Size
Presidents	Giant	8 ½	52
Pitas	Toro	6 ⅛	50
Casa Grande	Churchill	7 ¼	46
No. 75	Corona	5 ½	44
Largo Elegantes	Slim Panatela	7	32
Diademas	Double Corona	7 ¼	54
Superiors	Robusto	5 ½	48
Chateau Lafitte	Double Corona	7 ¼	54
Britania	Toro	6 ¼	50
Seleccion Deluxe			
Chateau "L"	Double Corona	7 ¼	54
Chateau "M"	Corona Extra	5 ¾	46
Coronas	Grand Corona	6 ¼	45
Grand Cru Seleccion			
Diademas	Doubaale Corona	7 ¼	54
Monarcas (tubed)	Churchill	6 ¾	48
Prince Consorts	Giant	8 ½	52

Country Cuba

Flavor Mild

Quality Superior

Distinctions Rafael Gonzalez is a brand
that was created in 1928 especially for
the British market. Indeed, the company invented the Lonsdale especially for
the Earl of Lonsdale. One of its unusual characteristics is the box, which car-
ries these words: "These cigars have
been manufactured from a secret blend
of pure Vuelta Abajo tobaccos selected
by the Marquez Rafael Gonzalez,
Grandee of Spain. For more than 20
years this brand existed. In order that
the connoisseur may fully appreciate
the perfect fragrance they should be
smoked either within one month of the
date of shipment from Havana or
should be carefully matured for about
one year." These cigars are light for
Cubans but have a rich flavor.

Panatelas

Cigar	Category	Length	Ring Size
Lonsdale	Lonsdale	6 $\frac{1}{2}$	42
Coronas Extra	Corona Extra	5 $\frac{5}{8}$	46
Petit Lonsdales	Petit Corona	5 $\frac{1}{16}$	42
Petit Coronas	Petit Corona	5 $\frac{1}{16}$	42
Panatelas	Small Panatela	4 $\frac{9}{16}$	34
Slenderellas	Slim Panatela	6 $\frac{7}{8}$	28

RAMON ALLONES

Country Cuba

Flavor Full bodied with strong aroma.

Quality Superior

Distinctions Ramon Allones came from Spain to make cigars in 1837 and founded the second-oldest Cuban brand. He brought with him several innovative ideas, among them the use of colorful labels on his boxes. The history of cigars would not be the same without them. He also invented the 8-9-8 method of packing cigars, on the theory that the cigars would stay more rounded in the box because there would be less pressure in the rows. Roman Allones cigars, not for beginners, are favorites with connoisseurs who appreciate the full-bodied flavor.

Toppers

Cigar	Category	Length	Ring Size
Gigantes	Double Corona	7 5/8	49
Churchill 8-9-8	Grand Corona	6 3/4	43
Coronas 8-9-8	Corona	5 9/16	42
Petit Coronas	Petit Corona	5 1/16	42
Ramonitas	Small Panatela	5	35
Toppers	Corona	6	40

RAMON ALLONES

Country Dominican Republic

Flavor Mild to medium bodied with a hint of coffee flavor.

Quality Superior 🌿🌿🌿

Distinctions The Dominican Ramon Allones has a filler blend of Jamaican, Dominican, and Mexican tobaccos, a Mexican binder, and a Cameroon wrapper. These cigars are much milder than the Havanas that bear this name. The Crystals come in individual glass tubes. And the Trumps are packed in a cedar box without a band or cellophane.

Cigar	Category	Length	Ring Size
D	Petit Corona	5	42
A	Lonsdale	6 1/2	42
Redondos	Double Corona	7	49
Crystals (tubed)	Lonsdale	6 3/4	42
Trumps	Lonsdale	6 3/4	43

Trumps

ROMEO Y JULIETA

Country Cuba

Flavor Medium bodied with rich, complex flavor.

Quality Superior

Distinctions Passion for each other was the downfall of Romeo and Juliet, but passion for cigars created the success of Romeo y Julieta, the brand that Rodriguez "Pepin" Fernandez made famous. In 1903 the founder bought a small company, and within two years built the Romeo y Julieta name into the largest-selling premium Havana cigar in the world. He elevated the brand to the aristocracy by creating personalized cigar bands for royalty, heads of state and important personages, printing thousands of one-of-a-kind bands. Today Romeo y Julieta is one of Cuba's most famous brands, the producer of forty-six models of cigars both handmade and machine-made. Because of this large number, not every one is as good as the best, but the very good are extraordinary.

Cigar	Category	Length	Ring Size
Fabulosos	Grand Corona	9 1/2	47
Prince of Wales	Churchill	7	27
Clemenceaus	Churchill	7	47
Cedros de Luxe No. 1	Lonsdale	6 1/2	42
Cazadores	Grand Corona	6 3/8	44
Romeo No. 2 de Luxe	Petit Corona	5 1/16	42
Shakespeares	Slim Panatela	6 7/8	28
Exhibicion No. 3	Corona Extra	5 5/8	46
Petit Julietas	Cigarillo	3 6/16	30

Prince of Wales

ROMEO Y JULIETA

Country Dominican Republic

Flavor Medium bodied, flavorful and aromatic.

Quality Superior 🍃 🍃 🍃

Distinctions The Dominican Romeo y Julieta has a Dominican and Cuban seed filler, a Connecticut broad leaf binder, and a Cameroon wrapper. The brand's standout is the Vintage series, which has an outstanding silky Connecticut shade wrapper, a Cuban seed and Dominican filler, and an aged Mexican binder, a combination that produces an unusually cultivated taste. These cigars are packed in a Spanish cedar box, fitted with a French Credo humidifier.

Cigar	Category	Length	Ring Size
Romeos	Pyramid	6	46
Chiquitas	Small Panatela	4 1/4	32
Delgados	Slim Panatela	7	32
Palmas	Long Corona	6	43
Romeo y Julieta Vintage			
I	Long Corona	6	43
III	Robusto	4 1/4	50
IV	Churchill	7	48
VI	Giant	7	60

Romeos

ROYAL DOMINICANA

Country Dominican Republic

Flavor Mild to medium bodied.

Quality Excellent

Distinctions Royal Dominicana cigars are well-constructed and affordable. Their filler is Dominican, binder Mexican, and wrapper Connecticut. The combination produces a mild to medium-bodied cigar, which is sold exclusively to J.R. Tobacco.

Super Fino

Cigar	Category	Length	Ring Size
Churchill	Double Corona	7 1/4	50
Nacional	Corona	5 1/2	43
Corona	Grand Corona	6	46
No. 1	Lonsdale	6 3/4	43
Super Fino	Panatela	6	35

ROYAL JAMAICA

Country Dominican Republic

Flavor Mild.

Quality Superior

Distinctions Jamaica was the home of this brand until destruction caused by Hurricane Hugo in 1989 forced the company to move. Relocating in the Dominican Republic, the owners still use a filler featuring Jamaican tobacco blended with Dominican, a Java binder, and a Cameroon wrapper. One of the best mild cigars, Royal Jamaica's maduro series is more full bodied with an added sweetness imparted by the dark Mexican wrapper.

Tube No. 1

Cigar	Category	Length	Ring Size
Navarro	Slim Panatela	6 3/4	34
Director No. 1	Grand Corona	6	45
Doubloon	Slim Panatela	7	30
Park Lane	Grand Corona	6	47
Rapier	Cigarillo	6 1/2	28
Royal Corona	Long Corona	6	40
Tube No. 1	Lonsdale	6 1/2	42
Royal Jamaica Maduro			
Churchill	Giant	8	51
Corona Grande	Lonsdale	6 1/2	42
Corona	Corona	5 1/2	40
Buccaneer	Slim Panatela	5 1/2	30

SAINT LUIS REY

Country Cuba

Flavor Full-bodied with refined flavor and aroma.

Quality Superior 🍃🍃🍃

Distinctions Saint Luis Rey are among the best Cuban cigars and an excellent value. Created fifty years ago for the British market, the brand is attractively presented in a white box with gold edging and a red label. They should not be mistaken for cigars of the San Luis Rey label, which are made in Cuba for German consumption and also machine made in Germany. These have a green and gold label with the same design. A limited production maintains the high quality of these cigars, which are intended for connoisseurs.

Serie A

Cigar	Category	Length	Ring Size
Double Corona	Double Corona	$7\,5/8$	49
Churchill	Churchill	7	47
Lonsdale	Lonsdale	$6\,1/2$	42
Serie A	Corona Extra	$5\,5/8$	46
Regios	Robusto	5	48
Coronas	Corona	$5\,9/16$	42
Petit Corona	Petit Corona	$5\,1/16$	42

SANCHO PANZA

Country Cuba

Flavor Mild with flavorful aroma.

Quality Superior

Distinctions Sancho Panza is an old Cuban brand whose mild but complex flavor makes it almost too much for a beginner, but not enough for an experienced smoker. However, these are interesting cigars and deserve a place in both repertoires. Therefore, Sancho Panza seems best as a daytime cigar for regular smokers. For newcomers they offer a good range to experiment with. They are most widely available in Spain.

Dorados

Cigar	Category	Length	Ring Size
Sanchos	Grand Corona	9 $\frac{1}{2}$	47
Coronas Gigantes	Churchill	7	47
Molinos	Lonsdale	6 $\frac{1}{2}$	42
Dorados	Lonsdale	6 $\frac{1}{2}$	42
Belicosos	Figurado	5 $\frac{1}{2}$	52
Bachillers	Half Corona	4 $\frac{9}{16}$	40

SANTA CLARA

Country Mexico

Flavor Mild to medium flavor.

Quality Excellent 🍃🍃

Distinctions Santa Clara, which has the date of its founding, 1830, on its band, is an all-Mexican cigar. All tobaccos, filler, binder, and wrapper, which is Sumatra seed, are Mexican grown. The unique flavor is imparted by the wrapper, which offers a choice, in most sizes, of natural or maduro shades.

III

Cigar	Category	Length	Ring Size
I	Double Corona	7	52
III	Lonsdale	$6\,^5/_8$	43
V	Long Corona	6	44
VII	Cigarillo	$5\,^1/_2$	25
Premier Tubes (tubed)	Panatela	$6\,^3/_4$	38
Quino	Small Panatela	$4\,^1/_2$	30

SANTA DAMIANA

Country Dominican Republic

Flavor Mild to medium bodied.

Quality Superior 🍃 🍃 🍃

Distinctions The name Santa Damiana is a resurrection of an old Cuban brand recreated for the contemporary smoker. Only in production since 1992, the cigars are made in a modern factory in the Dominican Republic and blended with today's sophisticated smoker in mind. The filler is a blend of Mexican and Dominican tobaccos, the binder is Mexican, and the wrapper is an especially fine Connecticut leaf. Different blends and names are made for the United States and European markets.

Cigar	Category	Length	Ring Size
Seleccion No. 100	Churchill	6 ¾	48
Seleccion No. 300	Corona Extra	5 ½	46
Seleccion No. 500	Robusto	5	50
Seleccion No. 700	Lonsdale	6 ½	42
Seleccion No. 800	Double Corona	7	50

Seleccion No. 800

SOSA

Country Dominican Republic

Flavor Medium to full bodied.

Quality Good

Distinctions Juan Sosa created this brand in the 1970s, and the current range attempts to bring the taste up to date. The fillers in these cigars are Dominican and Brazilian, and the binders are Honduran. In keeping with this international cast, the wrappers are either Sumatra seed, Ecuadorian grown, or aged Connecticut broad leaf. The cigars are attractively priced.

Governor

Cigar	Category	Length	Ring Size
Wavell	Robusto	4 ³/₄	50
Brevas	Corona	5 ¹/₂	43
Piramide No. 2	Pyramid	7	64
Santa Fe	Panatela	6	35
Magnums	Double Corona	7 ¹/₂	52
Governor	Toro	6	50

SUERDIECK

Country Brazil

Flavor Mild to medium.

Quality Good

Distinctions Suerdieck, the best-known Brazilian brand, makes a large number of cigars, more machine made than hand-made. Almost all use home-grown tobaccos, although a few combine Sumatra seed/Brazilian-grown leaf. Most models have small ring gauges. Although some smokers find the flavor appealing, the quality could be better.

Brasilia

Cigar	Category	Length	Ring Size
Brasilia	Slim Panatela	5 $\frac{1}{2}$	30
Finos	Grand Corona	5 $\frac{3}{4}$	46
Viajantes	Petit Corona	5	40
Corona Brasil Luxo	Corona Extra	5 $\frac{1}{2}$	42
Mata Fina Especial	Corona	5 $\frac{1}{4}$	42

TE-AMO

Country Mexico

Flavor Mild to medium.

Quality Good

Distinctions Te-Amo means "I love you" in Spanish, and in the United States this is the most beloved Mexican brand. The cigars are made in the San Andres Valley, where the tobaccos flourish, and this home-grown effort is a considerable enterprise. Although the cigars are mild to begin with, most are available in a choice of light or medium in wrappers of natural or maduro.

Torito

Cigar	Category	Length	Ring Size
Celebration (tubed)	Lonsdale	6 5/8	44
Gran Piramides	Pyramid	7 3/4	54
Satisfaction	Grand Corona	6	46
Caballero	Long Panatela	7	35
Torito	Robusto	4 3/4	50
Presidente	Double Corona	7	50
Elegante	Cigarillo	5 3/4	27
CEO	Giant	8 1/2	52
Relaxation	Lonsdale	6 5/8	44

TEMPLE HALL

Country Jamaica

Flavor Mild to medium with subtle spice.

Quality Excellent 🍃🍃

Distinctions Temple Hall is named for a Jamaican tobacco plantation founded by Cubans in 1876, but the name lapsed until it was revived in 1992 with this line of cigars. Their filler is a blend of Jamaican, Dominican, and Mexican tobaccos, the binder is Mexican, and the wrapper is Connecticut shade leaf. Considering Macanudo as the standard for Jamaican cigars, these have more body, but are still subtle with a touch of spice and floral overtones.

685

Cigar	Category	Length	Ring Size
700	Double Corona	7	49
685	Panatela	6 $7/8$	34
500	Small Panatela	5	31
Trumps No. 1	Lonsdale	6 $1/2$	42
Trumps No. 3	Corona	5 $1/2$	42

TRESADO

Country Dominican Republic

Flavor Mild to medium.

Quality Excellent

Distinctions Tresado is a good cigar for a beginner, mild, affordable, and well made. The filler and binder are Dominican, and the Indonesian wrapper adds a touch of complexity to the flavor. There are only five selections in the line, but they offer an opportunity to try a good introductory range of sizes.

Seleccion No. 300

Cigar	Category	Length	Ring Size
Seleccion No. 100	Giant	8	52
Seleccion No. 200	Churchill	7	48
Seleccion No. 300	Grand Corona	6	46
Seleccion No. 400	Lonsdale	6 5/8	44
Seleccion No. 500	Corona	5 1/2	42

TRINIDAD

Country Cuba

Flavor Medium to full bodied.

Quality Superior

Distinctions This is what the world knows about Trinidad. The brand, or the cigar, because there is only one model, exists. The cigar has a simple gold band with "Trinidad" printed in black. One hundred-sixty-four people smoked the Trinidad at "The Dinner of the Century," given in Paris in 1994 by Marvin Shanken, publisher of *Cigar Aficionado*. The assumption is that the Trinidad was created for Fidel Castro, and only Castro, to present to visiting dignitaries. Castro has denied that he initiated such a project. Nonetheless, about twenty boxes of one-hundred Trinidads are produced each month at the El Laguito Factory. Someone in Cuba must know why.

Cigar	Category	Length	Ring Size
Mystery Cigar	?	?	?

VERACRUZ

Country Mexico

Flavor Mild to medium to spicy overtones.

Quality Superior 🍃🍃🍃

Distinctions Veracruz, named for the Mexican state where the San Andres tobacco growing valley is located, is a premium cigar with a mild flavor. Founded in 1977 by Oscar J. Franck Terrazas, it is distributed primarily in the Continental United States and Hawaii. The brand's outstanding feature is its packaging. The glass tubes that encase Veracruz's larger sizes are like mini-humidors, sealed with foam and a rubber stopper, then wrapped in tissue and packed in an individual cedar box. The price is commensurate with the packaging, but the freshness of the cigars is justifiably guaranteed.

Cigar	Category	Length	Ring Size
Flor de Veracruz Carinas	Small Panatela	$4\,5/8$	34
Mina de Veracruz (tubed)	Long Corona	$6\,1/4$	42
Pemas de Veracruz (tubed)	Lonsdale	$6\,1/4$	42
Veracruz Magnum (tubed)	Churchill	$7\,7/8$	48

ZINO

Country Honduras

Flavor **Standard Series:** Medium.
Mouton-Cadet Series: Mild.
Connoisseur Series: Full bodied.

Quality Superior 🍃🍃🍃

Distinctions Zino was founded by cigar guru Zino Davidoff (see Davidoff) in the late 1970s. With the name "Zino," no one is going to question the quality of

Mouton Cadet Series No. 1

Diamond

these cigars. There are three series, the Standard, the Mouton-Cadet, created with the Baronne Philippine de Rothschild in mind, and the Connoisseur Series, launched to mark the opening of a Davidoff's store in New York. The filler and binder in all three categories are Honduran tobaccos, and the wrapper is the finest Connecticut shade leaf.

Cigar	Category	Length	Ring Size
Princesse	Cigarillo	4 1/4	20
Diamond	Corona	5 1/2	40
Tradition	Lonsdale	6 1/4	44
Elegance	Panatela	6 3/4	34
Veritas	Double Corona	7	50
Zino Mouton-Cadet Series			
No. 1	Lonsdale	6 1/2	44
No. 2	Panatela	6	35
No. 5	Petit Carona	5	42
No. 6	Robusto	5	50
Connoisseur Series			
Connoisseur 100	Double Corona	7 3/4	50
Connoisseur 200	Churchill	7 1/2	46
Connoisseur 300	Grand Corona	5 3/4	46

MASS MARKET CIGARS:
A Listing

The "mass" in mass market refers both to the machine-made process, and to the mass marketing of the cigars. Five to eight-hundred cigars produced by a machine in one minute certainly deserve the description "mass," and so do the millions that are sold. Most of the these companies use short filler tobacco, and homogenized tobacco for the binder and sometimes for the wrapper. The greatest strength of these cigars is their consistency.

List of Mass Market Brands

Antonio y Cleopatra
Arango Sportsman
William Ascot
As You Like It
B-H
Bances
Ben Bey
Ben Franklin
Black & Mild
Black Hawk
Brazil
Budd Sweet
Caribbean Rounds
Celestino Vega
Charles Denby
Charles the Great
Cherry Blend
The Cigar Baron
J. Cortes
Cyrilla
Dester Londres
Directors
Don Cesar
Dry Slitz
R. G. Dunn
Dutch Masters
1886
El Cauto
El Macco
El Producto

El Trelles
El Verso
Emerson
Evermore
Farnam Drive
Figaro
Florida
Garcia y Vega
Gargoyle
Gold & Mild
Harvester
Hauptmann's
Havana Blend
Hav-A-Tampa
Ibold
Jon Piedro
Jose Melendi
J. R. Famous
Keep Moving
King Edward
La Fendrich
Lancer
Lord Beaconsfield
Marsh
Muniemaker
Muriel
Nat Cicco's
Odin
Old Hermitage
Optimo
Palma

Pancho Garcia
Pedro Iglesias
Phillies
Pollack
Red Dot
Rigoletto
Robert Burns
Roi-Tan
Rosedale
San Christobal
San Felice
Santa Fe
San Vicente
Sierra Sweet
'63 Air-Flo
Swisher Sweets
Tampa Cub
Tampa Nugget
Tampa Sweet
Topper
Topstone
Travis Club
Villa de Cuba
Villazon Deluxe
White Owl
William Penn
Windsor & Mark IV
Wolf Bros.
Y. B.
Zino

ANTONIO Y CLEOPATRA
Country Puerto Rico

Cigar	Category	Length	Ring Size
Grenadiers Whiffs	Cigarillo	$3\,^5/_8$	$23\,^2/_3$
Grenadiers			
Palma Maduro	Corona	$5\,^5/_8$	$42\,^1/_2$
Panatela Deluxe	Panatela	$5\,^3/_8$	$35\,^1/_2$
Grenadiers	Slim Panatela	$6\,^1/_4$	$33\,^1/_2$
Connecticut Shade Wrapper Series			
Grenadiers Miniatures	Cigarillo	$4\,^1/_2$	28
Grenadiers Panatelas	Panatela	$5\,^3/_8$	$35\,^1/_2$
Grenadiers Presidentes	Corona	$5\,^5/_8$	$42\,^1/_2$

ARANGO SPORTSMAN
Country United States

Cigar	Category	Length	Ring Size
No. 100	Slim Panatela	$5\,^3/_4$	34
No. 200	Lonsdale	$6\,^1/_4$	42
No. 300	Churchill	7	46
No. 350	Robusto	$5\,^3/_4$	48

WM. ASCOT
Country United States

Cigar	Category	Length	Ring Size
Palma	Lonsdale	$6\,^1/_4$	42
Rounds	Churchill	7	46
Panatela	Slim Panatela	$5\,^3/_4$	34

AS YOU LIKE IT
Country United States

Cigar	Category	Length	Ring Size
No. 18	Long Corona	6	41
No. 22	Petit Corona	4 1/2	41
No. 32	Long Corona	6	43

B-H
Country United States

Cigar	Category	Length	Ring Size
Boston Blunts	Lonsdale	6 1/2	42
Golden Grande	Panatela	6 1/2	36
Esceptionales	Robusto	5 1/2	50

BANCES
Country United States

Cigar	Category	Length	Ring Size
Crowns	Robusto	5 3/4	50
Havana Holders	Slim Panatela	6 1/2	30
No. 3	Grand Corona	5 3/4	46

CARIBBEAN ROUNDS
Country United States

Cigar	Category	Length	Ring Size
Casinos	Lonsdale	6 1/2	43
Petites	Short Panatela	4 5/8	36
Rounds	Lonsdale	7 1/4	45

CELESTINO VEGA

Country United States

Cigar	Category	Length	Ring Size
The Islander	Petite Corona	5 $\frac{3}{4}$	48
Classic Stogie	Slim Panatela	7	34
Poquito	Cigarillo	4 $\frac{1}{4}$	24

CHARLES THE GREAT

Country United States
Machine-made with long filler

Cigar	Category	Length	Ring Size
Churchill	Double Corona	7	50
English Rounds	Long Corona	6	43
Classic	Panatela	6	34

J. CORTES

Country Belgium
Machine-made with one-hundred percent tobacco

Cigar	Category	Length	Ring Size
Long Filer No. 1	Panatela	5 $\frac{1}{2}$	38
Milord	Small Panatela	4 $\frac{1}{4}$	30
Mini	Cigarillo	3 $\frac{1}{3}$	19

DIRECTORS

Country United States

Cigar	Category	Length	Ring Size
Coronella	Cigarillo	5	27 $\frac{1}{2}$
Corona	Long Corona	6	44
Panatela	Short Panatela	5 $\frac{3}{8}$	36

R. G. DUNN

Country United States

Cigar	Category	Length	Ring Size
Babies	Petit Corona	4 $\frac{1}{8}$	42
Youngfellow	Slim Panatela	5 $\frac{1}{4}$	34
Bouquet	Corona	5 $\frac{1}{2}$	42 $\frac{1}{2}$

DUTCH MASTERS

Country Puerto Rico

Cigar	Category	Length	Ring Size
Cameroon Elite	Slim Panatela	6 $\frac{1}{8}$	29 $\frac{1}{2}$
President	Corona	5 $\frac{5}{8}$	40 $\frac{1}{2}$
Cadet Regular	Cigarillo	4 $\frac{3}{4}$	27 $\frac{1}{2}$
Belvedere	Corona Extra	4 $\frac{7}{8}$	46 $\frac{1}{2}$

EL CAUTO

Country Dominican Republic

Cigar	Category	Length	Ring Size
Blunt	Long Corona	6	43
Fumas	Grand Corona	6 $\frac{3}{8}$	46
Super Fumas	Lonsdale	4	44

EL PRODUCTO

Country Puerto Rico

Cigar	Category	Length	Ring Size
Little Coronas	Small Panatela	4 $\frac{5}{8}$	31
Blunts	Corona	5 $\frac{5}{8}$	40 $\frac{1}{2}$
Bouquets	Petit Corona	4 $\frac{3}{4}$	44
Favoritas	Robusto	5	48 $\frac{1}{2}$
Queens (tubed)	Corona	5 $\frac{5}{8}$	42

EL TRELLES

Country United States

Cigar	Category	Length	Ring Size
Bankers	Long Corona	6	43
Blunt Extra	Corona Extra	5 $^{1}/_{4}$	45
Tryangles Deluxe	Pyramid	5 $^{1}/_{4}$	45

EL VERSO

Country United States

Cigar	Category	Length	Ring Size
Bouquet Dark	Corona Extra	4 $^{3}/_{4}$	45
Commodore	Panatela	6	36
Mellow	Cigarillo	4 $^{1}/_{4}$	29

EVERMORE

Country United States

Cigar	Category	Length	Ring Size
Original	Corona Extra	4 $^{5}/_{8}$	45
Palma	Long Corona	6	42
Grand Corona	Grand Corona	5 $^{3}/_{4}$	47

GARCIA Y VEGA

Country United States

Cigar	Category	Length	Ring Size
Chicos	Cigarillo	4 $^{1}/_{4}$	27
Bravuras	Slim Panatela	5 $^{3}/_{8}$	34
Senators	Petit Corona	4 $^{1}/_{2}$	41
Delgado Panatela	Short Panatela	5 $^{3}/_{8}$	34
Gallantes	Panatela	6 $^{3}/_{8}$	34
Napoleons	Corona	5 $^{3}/_{4}$	41
Crystals No. 200 (tubed)	Long Corona	6 $^{1}/_{8}$	41

HAUPTMANN'S

Country United States

Cigar	Category	Length	Ring Size
Perfecto	Corona Extra	5 $\frac{1}{8}$	45
Broadleaf	Corona	5 $\frac{1}{4}$	43
Panatela	Panatela	5 $\frac{3}{4}$	38

HAVANA BLEND

Country United States
Machine-made with one-hundred percent
Cuban (1959 crop) tobacco

Cigar	Category	Length	Ring Size
Petit Corona	Short Panatela	4 $\frac{3}{4}$	38
Palma Fina	Cigarillo	6 $\frac{1}{2}$	29
Doubloon	Lonsdale	6 $\frac{1}{2}$	42
Churchill	Churchill	7	47

HAV-A-TAMPA

Country United States

Cigar	Category	Length	Ring Size
Blunt	Corona	5	43
Cheroot	Small Panatela	4 $\frac{3}{4}$	31
Jewel Black Gold	Cigarillo	5	29
Perfecto	Petit Corona	4 $\frac{3}{4}$	43

IBOLD

Country United States

Cigar	Category	Length	Ring Size
Black Pete	Petit Corona	4 $\frac{7}{8}$	44
Breva	Robusto	5 $\frac{1}{8}$	51
Ideals	Panatela	5 $\frac{7}{8}$	38

JON PIEDRO

Country United States

Cigar	Category	Length	Ring Size
Acapulco Breva	Lonsdale	6 1/2	42
Acapulco Slims	Panatela	6 1/2	36
Broadleaf Rounds	Grand Corona	6 1/2	46

JOSE MELENDI

Country United States   Machine-made with long filler

Cigar	Category	Length	Ring Size
Vega I	Short Panatela	5 3/8	37
Vega VII	Lonsdale	7	35
Wild Maduro	Slim Panatela	6 7/8	34

KING EDWARD

Country United States

Cigar	Category	Length	Ring Size
Invincible Deluxe	Corona	5 1/2	42
Panatela Deluxe	Short Panatela	5 1/4	36
Little Cigars	Cigarillo	4 3/8	29

LORD BEACONSFIELD

Country United States

Cigar	Category	Length	Ring Size
Rounds	Churchill	7 1/4	46
Lords	Slim Panatela	7	34
Cubanola	Corona	5 1/2	44

MARSH

Country United States

Cigar	Category	Length	Ring Size
Mountaineer	Slim Panatela	5 $\frac{1}{2}$	34
Virginian	Panatela	5 $\frac{1}{2}$	37
Deluxe	Long Panatela	7	34

MUNIEMAKER

Country United States
Machine-made with one-hundred percent tobacco

Cigar	Category	Length	Ring Size
Regular	Corona Extra	4 $\frac{1}{2}$	47
Straight	Robusto	5 $\frac{1}{2}$	48
Judges Cave	Corona Extra	4 $\frac{1}{2}$	47

MURIEL

Country Puerto Rico

Cigar	Category	Length	Ring Size
Magnum	Corona Extra	4 $\frac{5}{8}$	46 $\frac{1}{2}$
Air Tips Regular (tipped)	Small Panatela	5	30 $\frac{1}{2}$
Coronella	Small Panatela	4 $\frac{5}{8}$	31
Coronella Sweet	Small Panatela	4 $\frac{5}{8}$	31

NAT CICCO'S

Country United States

Cigar	Category	Length	Ring Size
Churchill Rejects	Giant Corona	8	46
Governor	Long Corona	6	42
Jamaican Rounds	Churchill	7 $\frac{1}{4}$	46
Aromatic and Flavored Series			
Almond Liquer	Slim Panatela	6 $\frac{1}{2}$	34
Cuban Cafe	Slim Panatela	6 $\frac{1}{2}$	34
Plaza Aromatic	Long Corona	6	42

OPTIMO

Country United States

Cigar	Category	Length	Ring Size
Diplomat	Panatela	$6\,^1/_8$	33
Admiral	Long Corona	6	41
Sports	Petit Corona	$4\,^1/_2$	41

PEDRO IGLESIAS

Country United States

Cigar	Category	Length	Ring Size
Crowns	Corona Extra	5	45
Regents	Long Corona	6	44
Lonsdales	Lonsdale	$6\,^1/_2$	44

PHILLIES

Country United States

Cigar	Category	Length	Ring Size
Perfecto	Corona	$5\,^3/_4$	43
Titan	Long Corona	$6\,^1/_4$	44
Panatela	Slim Panatela	$5\,^1/_2$	34
King Cheroot	Slim Panatela	$5\,^1/_2$	32
Sweets	Corona	$5\,^3/_4$	43

RIGOLETTO

Country Puerto Rico

Cigar	Category	Length	Ring Size
Londonaire	Long Corona	$6\,^1/_4$	43
Black Jack	Corona Extra	$5\,^3/_8$	46
Palma Grande	Long Corona	6	41

ROI-TAN

Country Puerto Rico

Cigar	Category	Length	Ring Size
Bankers	Petit Corona	5	40 $\frac{1}{2}$
Falcons	Slim Panatela	6 $\frac{1}{4}$	33 $\frac{1}{2}$
Tips	Cigarillo	5 $\frac{1}{8}$	27

SANTA FE

Country United States

Cigar	Category	Length	Ring Size
Biltmore	Long Corona	6	41
Panatela	Slim Panatela	5 $\frac{1}{4}$	33
Patties	Corona	5 $\frac{1}{2}$	42

SWISHER SWEETS

Country United States

Cigar	Category	Length	Ring Size
Kings	Corona	5 $\frac{1}{2}$	42
Perfecto	Petit Corona	5	41
Outlaw	Small Panatela	4 $\frac{3}{4}$	32

TAMPA NUGGET

Country United States

Cigar	Category	Length	Ring Size
Sublime	Petit Corona	4 $\frac{3}{4}$	43
Tip Sweet (tipped)	Cigarillo	5	28
Juniors	Small Panatela	4 $\frac{1}{2}$	31

TAMPA SWEET

Country United States

Cigar	Category	Length	Ring Size
Perfecto	Petit Corona	4 3/4	43
Cheroot	Small Panatela	4 3/4	31
Tip Cigarillo (tipped)	Cigarillo	5	28

TOPPER

Country United States

Cigar	Category	Length	Ring Size
Grande Corona	Long Corona	6	44
Breva	Corona Extra	5 1/2	45
Ebony	Corona	5 1/2	44

TOPSTONE

Country United States

Cigar	Category	Length	Ring Size
Connecticut Broad Leaf Series			
Supreme	Long Corona	6	42
Extra Oscuro	Corona Extra	5 1/2	46
Directors	Churchill	7 3/4	47
Natural Dark Series			
Executives	Churchill	7 1/4	47
Panatela	Panatela	6	39

TRAVIS CLUB

Country United States

Cigar	Category	Length	Ring Size
Churchill	Double Corona	7	50
Centennial	Lonsdale	6 7/8	45
Toro	Toro	6	50

VILLA DE CUBA

Country United States

Cigar	Category	Length	Ring Size
Brevas	Corona	5 $\frac{3}{4}$	44
Majestics	Long Corona	6 $\frac{3}{8}$	43
Corona Grande	Giant Corona	7 $\frac{1}{4}$	45

WHITE OWL

Country United States

Cigar	Category	Length	Ring Size
Coronetta	Cigarillo	4 $\frac{5}{8}$	29
Demi-Tip (tipped)	Short Panatela	4 $\frac{1}{4}$	32
Miniatures Sweet	Cigarillo	4 $\frac{5}{8}$	29
Invincible	Corona	5 $\frac{5}{8}$	41
New Yorker	Corona	5 $\frac{5}{8}$	41
Blunts	Petit Corona	4 $\frac{3}{4}$	41
Ranger	Slim Panatela	6 $\frac{3}{8}$	34

WILLIAM PENN

Country United States

Cigar	Category	Length	Ring Size
Willow Tips (tipped)	Cigarillo	4 $\frac{1}{4}$	26
Perfecto	Corona	5 $\frac{3}{8}$	41
Panatela	Slim Panatela	5 $\frac{1}{4}$	34

WINDSOR & MARK IV

Country United States

Cigar	Category	Length	Ring Size
Crooks	Petit Corona	5	40
Maduro	Lonsdale	6 $\frac{1}{2}$	43
Panatela	Slim Panatela	6 $\frac{1}{2}$	34

WOLF BROS.

Country United States

Cigar	Category	Length	Ring Size
Nippers	Cigarillo	3 1/4	20
Crookettes	Small Panatela	4 1/2	32
Sweet Vanilla Crooks	Corona	5 1/2	42

ZINO

Country Brazil, the Netherlands, and Switzerland
Machine-made of one-hundred percent tobacco

Cigar	Category	Length	Ring Size
Made in Brazil			
Santos	Panatela	6 1/2	34
Por Favor	Small Panatela	4	30
Made in the Netherlands			
Drie Cello	Corona	5 3/4	40
Cigarillos Brasil	Cigarillo	3 1/2	20
Made in Switzerland			
Relax Brasil	Slim Panatela	5 3/4	30
Classic Sumatra	Petit Corona	4 3/4	41

SMALL CIGARS:
A Sampling

S mall cigars are a brief treat, and they can be excellent. Given the right circumstances, they can be an indispensable addition to anyone's cigar choices. All types of companies make small cigars, handmade and machine made, and the following lists are meant as a guide to what is available. The categories are as follows: Handmade brands that offer small cigars; machine-made brands that make small cigars; and those companies whose production is primarily small cigars. Of these companies, a few of the most prominent are described with some of their models.

Handmade brands
that include small cigars:

Andujara
Antelo
Belinda
Celestino Vega
Davidoff
Don Diego
El Rey del Mundo
Excalibur
Honduras Cuban Tobaccos
Hoyo de Monterrey
Iracema
Jose Benito
Juan Clemente
La Gloria Cubana
La Native
Macanudo

Montecruz
Nat Sherman
Off Colors
Oscar
Partagas
Pleiades
Pride of Copan
Primo del Rey
Private Stock
Punch
Royal Jamaica
Santa Clara
Suerdieck
Te-Amo
Upmann
Zino

Machine-made brands
that include small cigars:

Antonio y Cleopatra
Celestino Vega
J. Cortes
Directors
R. G. Dunn
Dutch Masters

El Verso
Garcia y Vega
Havana Blend
Hav-A-Tampa
Ibold
King Edward

Muriel
Phillies
Robert Burns
Roi-Tan
Swisher Sweets
Tampa Nugget

Tampa Sweet
White Owl
William Penn
Wolf Bros.
Zino

Machine-made brands
that predominately make small cigars:

Agio
Alamo
G. A. Andron
Al Capone
Avanti
Backwoods
Between the Acts
Captain Black
Christian of Denmark
Dannemann
Davidoff Cigarillos
Denobili
Ducados
Dunhill Small Cigars
Dutch Treats
Erik
Gesty
Gold Seal
Hamlet Slims
Henri Winterman
Indiana Slims
LaCorona
Madison

Manikin
Nobel Cigars
Omega
Panter
Parodi
Pedroni
Petri
Prince Albert
Rustlers
Sam Houston Special
Schimmelpenninck
Suerdieck
Supre Sweets
Super Value Little Cigars
Tijuana Smalls
Tiparillo
The Tobacconist Choice
Tobajara
Victoria
Villiger
Willem II Cigars
Winchester Little Cigars

EXAMPLES OF
MAJOR SMALL CIGAR BRANDS

VILLIGER

Country Switzerland

Distinctions Jean Villiger began making his own cigars in Switzerland in 1888. The company is now an empire still run by his family. The Villiger descendants oversee the production of over four hundred million cigars in Switzerland, Germany, and Ireland, which are exported to over seventy countries. All the cigars are machine-made now, and some use homogenized tobacco, but many are made with the finest aged tobaccos from Columbia, the Dominican Republic, Java, Mexico, and Cameroon.

Cigar	Category	Length	Ring Size*
Bunte (tipped)	Cigarillo	4 ½	
Curly	Cigarillo	7	
Villiger-Kiel Mild (tipped)	Cigarillo	6 ½	
Villiger Export	Cigarillo	4	
Villiger Export Kings	Cigarillo	5 ⅛	
Villiger Premium No.4	Cigarillo	4	
Rillos (tipped)	Cigarillo	4 ½	
Braniff No.1	Cigarillo	3 ½	
Braniff Cortos Filter Light	Cigarillo	3	

*Ring sizes not available from manufacturer.

AGIO

Country The Netherlands

Distinctions Agio is a brand of excellent quality that makes the "dry" Dutch type of cigars. Extremely popular in Europe, the cigars are made with tobaccos from Java, Sumatra, and Cameroon. The Mehari's, are found all over the Continent, but especially in Belgium and Germany.

Cigar	Category	Length	Ring Size
Biddies Brazil	Cigarillo	3 ¼	20
Mehari's Sumatra	Cigarillo	4	23
Mahari's Mild & Light	Cigarillo	4	23
Filter Tip (tipped)	Cigarillo	3	21
Senoritas Red Label	Small Panatela	4	21

DANNEMANN

Country Germany

Distinctions Dannemann is a venerable name in small cigars, having been established in 1873 by Geraldo Dannemann originally in Brazil. The cigars are made with Sumatra and Brazil tobaccos and are sold worldwide.

Cigar	Category	Length	Ring Size
Lights-Sumatra	Slim Panatela	6	34
Espada-Brazil	Corona Extra	5	45
Slims-Sumatra	Cigarillo	6 $\frac{1}{2}$	28
Moods	Cigarillo	2 $\frac{7}{8}$	20
Sweets	Cigarillo	3 $\frac{5}{8}$	20
Speciale-Brazil	Cigarillo	2 $\frac{7}{8}$	25
Imperial-Sumatra	Cigarillo	4 $\frac{1}{4}$	25
Pierrot-Brazil	Cigarillo	3 $\frac{7}{8}$	28

SCHIMMELPENNINCK

Country The Netherlands

Distinctions The Schimmelpenninck name is the mark of a world-class cigar. Although manufactured in Holland, these cigars are sought after all over the world, and ninety percent of their numbers are exported. These Dutch type "dry" cigars are made with excellent blends of short filler tobacco from Indonesia, Brazil, Cameroon, and even Havana. The Duet is one of the most popular cigars in the world of its size.

Cigar	Category	Length	Ring Size
Florina	Cigarillo	3 $\frac{7}{8}$	26
Nostra	Cigarillo	2 $\frac{7}{8}$	27
Media	Cigarillo	3	26
Mono	Cigarillo	3 $\frac{3}{8}$	27
Vada	Cigarillo	3 $\frac{7}{8}$	30
Duet Brazil	Cigarillo	5 $\frac{5}{8}$	27
Havana Milds	Cigarillo	3	26

NOBEL

Country Denmark

Distinctions The largest cigar producer in Denmark, Nobel was founded in 1835 and is credited with creating the one-hundred percent mini-cigarillo market in Europe. The Nobel Petit, created in 1898, is one of the oldest brands in the world. The company also makes the Christian of Denmark brand, which is gaining in popularity worldwide.

Cigar	Category	Length	Ring Size
Petit Sumatra	Cigarillo	$3\,^3/_8$	20
Medium Panatela Sumatra	Cigarillo	$3\,^1/_2$	22
Grand Panatela Sumatra	Cigarillo	$5\,^1/_2$	28
Petit Carona	Cigarillo	$3\,^1/_2$	32
Petit Lights	Cigarillo	$3\,^3/_8$	20

MAKING A PURCHASE:
Cigar Sellers Worldwide

ALABAMA

Birmingham
Churchill's
The Briary

Huntsville
Humidor Pipe Shop

Mobile
Tinder Box

ALASKA

Anchorage
Pete's Tobacco Shop
Tobacco Cache

ARIZONA

Phoenix
Smoker's Knight Gallery
Stag Tobacconist
Ye Old Pipe Shoppe

Scottsdale
Ford & Haig Tobacconist
Hiland Trading Company

Tucson
Smoker's Haven

ARKANSAS

Little Rock
The Pie & Tobacco

Fort Smith
Taylor's Pipe & Tobacco

CALIFORNIA

Beverly Hills
Davidoff of Geneva
Alfred Dunhill of London

Los Angeles
Century City Tobacco
Kenny's Cellar
The Wine House
Politically Incorrect
  Tobacco & Gifts

Long Beach
Hiland's Gifts & Tobacco
Churchill's

Hollywood
Up in Smoke

San Diego
Liberty Tobacco
Vintage Wines Ltd.

San Francisco
Alfred Dunhill of London
Grant's Pipe Shop
Sherlock's Haven
Vendetta's

Santa Barbara
The Cigar Co.

COLORADO

Denver
Cigar & Tobacco World
Jerri's Tobacco Shops
Prince Philips

Fort Collins
Edward's Tobacco & Darts

CONNECTICUT

Greenwich
Tobacconist of Greenwich

Hartford
De La Concha of Hartford
The Tobacco Shop

New Haven
Owl Shop

DISTRICT
OF COLUMBIA

Georgetown Tobacco & Pipe
J. R. Tobacco
W. Curtis Draper

DELAWARE

Wilmington
Books & Tobacco Inc.
Tobacco Village

FLORIDA

Boca Raton
Bennington Tobacconist

Jacksonville
Edward's of San Marco
Smoke 'n' Snuff

Key West
Key West Havana Cigar
La Tabaqueria

Miami
Cuban Aliados Smoke Shop
El Credito Cigars
Smoke Shope
Tropical Tobacco

North Miami Beach
Laurenzo's

Orlando
Pipe & Pouch Smoke Shop

Palm Beach
Chesterfield Hotel Deluxe

Sarasota
The Smoke Shop

Tampa
Cammarata Cigar Co.
Edward's Pipe & Tobacco
Simons Market

GEORGIA

Atlanta
Royal Cigar Co.
Windfaire, Inc.
Cigar Villa

HAWAII

Honolulu
Don Pablo Smoke Shope
R. Field Co.

IDAHO

Boise
Sturman's Smoke Shop

Ketchum
Atkinson Market

ILLINOIS

Chicago
Iwan Ries & Co.
Jack Schwartz
Old Chicago Smoke Shop
Rubovits Cigar

INDIANA

Fort Wayne
Pipe & Tobacco Shop

Indianapolis
Pipe Puffer Smoke Shop
The Tobacco Shop

IOWA

Des Moines
David's

KANSAS

Kansas City
Cigar & Tobacco, Ltd.

Topeka
Churchills of Westridge

KENTUCKY

Lexington
Straus Tobacconist

Louisville
Kremer's Smoke Shop
Oxmore Smoke Shoppe

LOUISIANA

New Orleans
Dos Jefes
The Epitome

MAINE

Bangor
Stillwater Convenience

Portland
Joe's Smoke Shop
The Calabash

MARYLAND

Baltimore
Fink's Liquors
Wells Liquors

Annapolis
The Smoke Shop

MASSACHUSETTS

Boston
Alfred Dunhill of London
L. J. Peretti Co.
Two Guys Smoke Shop

Worcestor
The Cigar Merchant
The Owl Shop

MICHIGAN

Dearborn
Grill & Bar, Ritz Carlton
  Hotel
Detroit Area
Churchill's at Birmingham
Dearborn Tobacco Co.
Watkens Cigar
Humidor'One & Panache
J. R. Tobacco
Lil Havana

Lansing
Max Pipe & Tobacco

Saginaw
Austin's Fine Pipes &
  Tobacco
Daves Smokin' Post

MINNESOTA

Minneapolis/St. Paul Area
L & M Smoke Shop
Golden Leaf Ltd.
Lewis Pipe & Tobacco
C & W Coffee & Tobacco

MISSISSIPPI

Biloxi
The Epitome
The Smoke Shop, Ltd.

MISSOURI

Kansas City Area
Mr. Tobacco

St. Louis
Briars & Blends

MONTANA

Billings
Tinder Box

NEBRASKA

Lincoln
Ted's Tobacco

Omaha
David's Briar Shop
Nickleby's Smoke Ring

NEVADA

Las Vegas
Churchill's Tobacco
  Emporium
Don Pablo Cigar Co.
Las Vegas Cigar Co.
Mr. Bill's Pipe & Tobacco Co.
Reno
Tinder Box

NEW HAMPSHIRE

Laconia
Happy Jack's Pipe &
  Tobacco

NEW JERSEY

Newark Area
The Chatham Wine Shop,
  Chatham
Smoker's World, Ltd.,
  Englewood
Burns Tobacco, Fairlawn
Cuban Aliados, Union City
Westfield Pipe Shop,
  Westfield
Southern New Jersey Area
Hamilton News & Tobacco,
  Mays Landing
Delmonte's News Agency,
  Camden
Track Towne Smoke Shop,
  Cherry Hill

NEW MEXICO

Albuquerque
Stag Tobacconist of
  Albuquerque
Santa Fe
Palace Cigar

NEW YORK

Albany
Edleez Tobacco
W. J. Coulson
Long Island Area
Stan's Tobacco Emporium,
  Baldwin
Zubair Tobacco, Lawrence
Smoke Stax, New
  Hyde Park
Fortune Smoke Shop,
  Westbury

Rochester
Moretti's of San Francisco
Water Street Grill

New York City
Alfred Dunhill of London
Arnold's Tobacco Shop
Barclay-Rex, Inc.
Davidoff of Geneva
Home of Tobacco Products
J. R. Tobacco
Nat Sherman
De La Concha Tobacconist
Mom's Cigar Shop

Syracuse
Kieffers Cigar Store
Mallard Tobacconist

NORTH CAROLINA

Charlotte
The Humidor
McCranies Pipe Shop

Greensboro
Mr. Finnegan's Table

Raleigh
Tobacconist of Raleigh

Winston Salem
Pipes, Etc.

OHIO

Cincinnati
Cincinnati Tobacconist
Private Smoking Club

Cleveland
Huntington Building
    Cigar Store
Cousin Cigar Co.

Columbus
Barclay Pipe & Tobacco
Camelot Tobacco
P & A Cigars
Pipes & Pleasure

OKLAHOMA

Oklahoma City
Tobacco Exchange

Tulsa
Ted's Pipe Shop

OREGON

Portland Area
Timber Valley Tobaccos,
    Beaverton

Rich's Cigar Store, Portland
T. Whittaker Tobacco's,
    Portland

PENNSYLVANIA

Philadelphia
Chestnut Smoke Shop
Tobacco Village
Holts Cigar

Pittsburgh
Blooms Cigar Co.
Continental Smoke Shop
Poor Richards Freight
    House Shops

RHODE ISLAND

Providence
Jolly Roger's Smokeshop
Red Carpet Smoke Shop

SOUTH CAROLINA

Charleston
Smokey's Tobacco Shop

SOUTH DAKOTA

Sioux Falls
Eastwood Drug & Smoke

TENNESSEE

Knoxville
Smokin Joe's
Smoky's Pipes & Tobacco

Memphis
Tinder Box
Tobacco Corner

Nashville
Arcade Smoke Shop
Mosko's Inc.
Tobacco Road Smoke Shop

Chattanooga
Chattanooga Billiard Club

TEXAS

Austin
Gas Pipe Emporium
Texas Tobacconist
Wiggy's

Dallas
Alfred Dunhill of London
The Gas Pipe
Marty's

Tobacco Club Inc.
Up in Smoke

Houston
Antique Pipe Shoppe
Carol's Pipe Pub
Jeffrey Stone Ltd.
McCoy's Fine Cigars &
  Tobacco

San Antonio
The Humidor

El Paso
Papa's

UTAH

Salt Lake City
Tinder Box

VERMONT

Burlington
Garcia Tobacco Shop

Manchester
Vermont Pipe Shop

VIRGINIA

Richmond
Tobacco House Ltd.
Tobacconist of Richmond

Roanoke
Milan Bros.
Treasures Gift & Tobacco

Alexandria
John Crouch Tobacconist

McLean
Georgetown Tobacco & Pipe

Norfolk
Emerson's Fine Tobacco

WASHINGTON

Seattle
Arcade Smoke Shop
G & G Cigar Co.
Nickel Cigar
Tom's University
  Smoke Shop

WEST VIRGINIA

Charleston
The Squire

WISCONSIN

Milwaukee
Edward's Pipe & Tobacco
Uhle's Pipe Shop

Madison
The Tobacco Bar

WYOMING

Jackson
Tobacco Row

Moran
Jenny Lake Lodge Lounge

INTERNATIONAL

AUSTRALIA

Melbourne
Benjamins Fine Tobacco
Daniels Fine Tobacco

Sydney
Alfred Dunhill of London
Cigar Divan at Pierpoints
  Hotel Intercontinental

BELGIUM

Brussels
Le Roi du Cigare
Zabia

BRAZIL

Sao Paulo
Havana Cigars Comercio
Casa del Habana

CANADA

ALBERTA

Calgary
Cavendish & Moore's
  Tobacco Ltd.

BRITISH COLUMBIA

Vancouver
R. J. Clarke Tobacconists

ONTARIO

Ottawa
M. Comerford & Son Ltd.

Toronto
Havana Tobacconists
Thomas Hinds
  Tobacconists Ltd.
Winston & Holmes
  Tobacconists

QUEBEC

Montreal
Blatter & Blatter
Davidoff

Quebec City
J. E. Giguare Ltd.

CUBA

Havana
Casa del Habano • Partagas
  Cigar Factory
Casa del Habano • Tobacco
  Museum
Casa del Tabaro • Guitart-
  Habana Libre Hotel
Casa del Tabaco
Tienda de Tabaco •
  Comodoro Hotel

DENMARK

Copenhagen
Neils Larsen

FRANCE

Lyons
Le Khedive

Saint Tropez
Chez Fuchs

Paris
Tabac des Quatre Temps
A Casa del Habano
La Civette
Tabac La Tabagie
Tabac George V

GERMANY

Berlin
Horst Kiwus
Ka De We

Hamburg
Duske und Duske
Pfeifen Timm

Heidelberg
Tabak Bieler KG

Munich
Max Zechbauer
Wilhem Bader

GREECE

Athens
M. Balli

HONG KONG

Cohiba Cigar Divan •
  Mandarin Hotel
Davidoff

IRELAND

Dublin
J.J. Fox

ITALY

Rome
Carmigani
Sincato

LEBANON

Beirut
La Casa del Habano

LUXEMBOURG

Luxembourg
La Civette

MEXICO

Mexico City
La Casa del Fumador

MONACO

Monte Carlo
Le Louis XV • Hotel de Paris

NETHERLANDS

Amsterdam
Hajenius

SAUDIA ARABIA

Jeddah
Hotel Sands Shop
Hotel Sofitel Shop
La Casa del Habano

SOUTH AFRICA

Capetown
Cock 'n Bull
Scottish Piper
Wesley's

Johannesburg
H & H Tobacconist
Cale Tobacconists
Smoker's Den
Wesley's

SPAIN

Barcelona
Gimeno

Madrid
Gonzales de Linares

Santiago
Calle Alcala

SWITZERLAND

Geneva
Davidoff
Comptoirs du Rhone
Alfred Dunhill
Fradkoff Cigares

Zurich
Davidoff
Durr
Samuel Menzi Cigar
Tabak Schwarzenbach

UNITED KINGDOM

Bath
Frederick Tanner

Edinburgh
Herbert Love

Cambridge
Harrison & Simmonds

London
Alfred Dunhill
Benson & Hedges
Davidoff of London
Harrod's Ltd.
James J. Fox and Robert Lewis
Sautter of Mayfair
Selfridges

VIRGIN ISLANDS

St. Thomas
Fort Wines & Spirits

SMOKING IN PUBLIC:
Friendly Places Worldwide

ALABAMA

Birmingham
Basil's Grill & Wine Bar

Huntsville
Aunt Eunice's Country
    Kitchen

Mobile
Weichman's All Seasons

Tallassee
East Tallassee Café

ALASKA

Anchorage
Corsair

Fairbanks
Chena Hot Springs Resort

ARIZONA

Carefree
The Boulders

Phoenix
Christopher's Bistro
Etienne's Different
    Point of View
The Grill

Scottsdale
Marquessa • Scottsdale
    Princess Hotel
The Ritz-Carlton
Spazzizi
Mary Elaine's
    Phoenician Resort

Tucson
Anthony's in the Catalinas
Daniel's Restaurant
Plaza Café & Bar

ARKANSAS

Little Rock
Capitol Bar
The Capitol Hotel

CALIFORNIA

Beverly Hills
Peninsula Beverly Hills

Carmel
Rio Grill
Pacific's Edge Restaurant

Los Angeles
Bellini
Bistro Garden
Checkers
Mum's Restaurant
Rockenwagner

Hollywood
Musso & Frank
La Toque

Monterey
The Sardine Factory
The Whaling Station Inn

Napa Valley
Mustards Grill
Restaurant at Meadowood
Napa Valley Grille
Showley's at Miramonte

Newport Beach
Conservatory Lounge
Four Seasons
John Dominis Restaurant
The Ritz

Palo Alto
Empire Grill & Tap Room

Pasadena
Bistro 45
Parkway Grill

Sacramento
Mace's
Morton's of Chicago

San Diego
Baci's
The Crown Room • Hotel
    Del Coronado
Prego Ristorante

San Francisco
Carnelian Room
Elka Restaurant
Ernie's Restaurant
Masa's
The Park Grill • Park Hyatt
    Hotel

Santa Monica
Remi

Santa Barbara
Trattoria Mollie
Wine Cask

COLORADO

Denver
Creekside Grill
Palace Arms
Cherry Cricket

Copper Mountain
Copper Mountain Resort

Vail
The Left Bank Restaurant

Fort Collins
Nico's Catacombs Restaurant

CONNECTICUT

Centerbrook
Fine Bouche Restaurant

Cheshire
Callahan's

Greenwich
Greenwich Cigar Club

Hartford
Max on Main

New Haven
Bruxelles

Manchester
Cavey's Northern Italian
  Restaurant

Stamford
Park Place

Trumbull
Ashley's • The Marriot

Westport
The Meeting Street Grill

Waterbury
Bacco's Restaurant

Mystic
Flood Time

Washington
The Mayflower Inn

Litchfield
Tollgate Hill Inn

DISTRICT OF COLUMBIA

City Club of Washington, D.C.
Capitol Grill
Calvert Café
Jockey Club • Ritz Carlton
John Hay Room • Hay Adams
  Hotel

Roma Restaurant
Washington Grill

DELAWARE

Wilmington
Columbus Inn

Dover
Blue Coat Inn

FLORIDA

Amelia Island
Lobby Lounge • Ritz Carlton

Boca Raton
Boca Raton Hotel & Club
The Broken Sound Club

Ft. Lauderdale
Harbor Beach
The Marriot

Key West
Angler's Seafood House
Yakitori Restaurant

Longboat Key
The Colony Restaurant
The Colony Beach Hotel

Miami
Café Royal
Caffe Abbracci
Casa Juancho Restaurant
Grand Café • Grand Bay Hotel
Le Pavillon Restaurant

Miami Beach
The Strand

Naples
Eagle Creek Country Club

Orlando
Chris' House of Beef

Palm Beach
Chesterfield Hotel Delux

Sarasota
Chophouse Grill
Gecko's Grill & Pub

St. Petersburg
Parkers Landing
Marina Beach Ressort

Tampa
Bern's Steak House

GEORGIA

Atlanta
Bones Restaurant
The Mansion
Florencia • Occidental Grand
  Hotel
The Peachtree Club

HAWAII

Honolulu
Kapalua Bay Club
Hy's Steakhouse

Maui
Avalon

ILLINOIS

Chicago
Bice Restaurant
Carlucci
Chez Paul Restaurant
Como Inn
The Dining Room • The Ritz
  Carlton Hotel
Great Street Restaurant &
  Bar • Stouffer Renaissance
Sorriso
Spiaggia

INDIANA

Fort Wayne
Café Johnell
My Father's Place

Indianapolis
Graffiti's Keystone Grill
St. Elmo Steak House

South Bend
La Salle Grill

IOWA

Des Moines
801 Steak & Chop House
Wakonda Club

KANSAS

Kansas City
The Woodlands

Wichita
Scotch & Sirloin

KENTUCKY

Lexington
Coach House Restaurant

Louisville
Flagship Restaurant
The Oakroom • The Seelbach
  Hotel
Spa Restaurant • Hyatt
  Regency Hotel

LOUISIANA

Lafayette
Stroud's Steakhouse

New Orleans
Arnaud's
Brennan's
Court of Two Sisters
Emeril's
The Rib Room • Omni Royal
  Orleans Hotel
Polo Lounge • Windsor Court
  Hotel

MAINE

Bangor
The Greenhouse Restaurant
La Conque • The Manor Inn
Sarah's

MARYLAND

Baltimore
The Fishery Restaurant
L'Auberge Restaurant
The Prime Rib

Bethesda
Vagabond

Chevy Chase
Chevy Chase Club

Potomac
Old Angler's Inn

MASSACHUSETTS

Boston
Anthony's Pier 4
Biba Restaurant
Bristol Lounge
The Capital Grille
Grill 23 & Bar
Locke-Ober
Seasons • Bostonian Hotel

Cambridge
Upstairs at the Pudding

Cataumet
Chart Room

Lenox
Blantyre Hotel

MICHIGAN

Dearborn
Grill & Bar • Ritz Carlton
  Hotel

Detroit
Caucus Club
Durango Grill
Fonte d'Amore
Opus One
Pike Street Restaurant
Vivio's

Grand Rapids
Lakos on the Hill

Lansing
Hummingbirds

Mackinac Island
The Woods • Grand Hotel

Royal Oak
Madison's

MINNESOTA

Minneapolis
Cocolezzone
Huberts
Minneapolis Club
Town & Country Club

St. Paul
Chang O'Hara's Bistro
The St. Paul Hotel
Sweeney's Saloon

MISSISSIPPI

Natchez
The Burn

Vicksburg
Delta Point

MISSOURI

Kansas City
Café Allegro
Jasper's
Marco Polo's
Willow Creek Manor Bed
   & Breakfast

St. Louis
Al Baker's
Cardwell's
Dierdorf & Harts Steak House
Missouri Athletic Club
Noonday Club
Sonny's Bar & Grill

MONTANA

Billings
Golden Belle Saloon •
   Northern Hotel

Gallatin Gateway
Gallatin Gateway Inn

NEBRASKA

Lincoln
Top Hat

Omaha
Chelsea House Restaurant
Le Café De Paris

NEVADA

Las Vegas
Ballys Casino Resort
Caesars Palace Hotel
Desert Inn
Flamingo Hotel
Edgewater Hotel
Las Vegas Hilton
The Mirage Hotel
Maxim Hotel & Casino
Morton's of Chicago
Pamplemousse
Sands Resort Hotel & Casino
Stardust Hotel
Venetian Restaurant

Reno
Harrah's Steak House

NEW HAMPSHIRE

Ashland
Common Man

Laconia
Boatslip Restaurant

Exeter
The Inn of Exeter

Waterville Valley
Legends 1291

NEW JERSEY

Atlantic City
Bally's Grand Hotel & Casino
Brighton Steak House • Sands
   Hotel & Casino
Trump's Castle • Hotel &
   Casino

Bloomfield
Seven Hills Restaurant

Fort Lee
Memories Restaurant

Hoboken
Amanda's

Lyndhurst
La Casa Gagazoata

Princeton
Alchemist & Barrister

Ridgefield Park
Tony Van Clief's

Trenton
Bond Street Club
Diamond's
Pete Lorenzo's Café
La Gondola Restorante

Wayne
Red Fox Inn

CIGARS

PAUL GARMIRIAN "BOMBONES"
DOMINICAN REPUBLIC : COLORADO WRAPPER
3 1/2 BY 43
$9.00

ROMEO Y JULIETA "PANATELAS"
DOMINICAN REPUBLIC : CAMEROON WRAPPER
5 1/4 BY 35
$7.00

CUBITA "NUMBER 500"
DOMINICAN REPUBLIC : CONNECTICUT SHADE WRAPPER
5 1/2 BY 43
$8.00

PADRON "LONDRES" MADURO
NICARAGUA : CONNECTICUT BROADLEAF WRAPPER
5 1/2 BY 42
$5.00

FELIPE GREGORIO "SERENO"
HONDURAS : HONDURAN WRAPPER
5 3/4 BY 42
$10.00

ARTURO FUENTE "SELECCION D'OR CHURCHILL"
DOMINICAN REPUBLIC : CONNECTICUT SHADE WRAPPER
7 1/4 BY 48
$8.00

AVO "PYRAMID"
DOMINICAN REPUBLIC : CONNECTICUT SHADE WRAPPER
7 BY 36/54
$15.00

Cigar menu from
Granville Restaurant &
Lounge in New York City

NEW MEXICO

Albuquerque
Albuquerque Hilton

Santa Fe
Evergreen Restaurant #303
La Cantina

Taos
Adobe Bar • Taos Inn

NEW YORK

Albany
The Cantebury
Mansion Hill Inn
Nicole's Bistro

Ramsonville
Equinox Skyline

Lewiston
Riverside Inn

Garden City
Jonathan's American Grill

Chappaqua
Crabtree's Kittle House Inn

Bardonia
Lock, Stock & Barrel

Rochester
Moretti's of San Francisco
Water Street Grill

Sag Harbor
American Hotel

Roslyn
Bryant & Cooper Steakhouse

New York City
Allison on Dominick
Ansonia
An American Place
The Assembly Restaurant
The Bar • The Four Seasons
    Hotel
Beekman Bar and Books
Ben Benson's Steakhouse
Café Pierre • The Pierre
    Hotel
Campagna
Chanterelle
Gallagher's Steak House
Granville Restaurant &
    Lounge
Hudson River Club
La Caravelle
La Cité
Le Cirque
Le Madri
Mark's Restaurant and Bar
Moran's Restaurant
Oak Room • The Plaza Hotel
Piccola Venezia Ristorante
Remi
San Domenico
Smith & Wollensky
The 21 Club
The Water Club

Syracuse
Pascale Restaurant

NORTH CAROLINA

Charlotte
Crossroads
The Lamp Lighter Restaurant
University Place Restaurant

Greensboro
Mr. Finnegan's Table

Raleigh
The Capital City Club
Rovence Restaurant •
    Radisson Plaza Hotel

Kingston
House of Wang

OHIO

Cincinnati
Celestial Restaurant
Cricket
Maisonette
Montgomery Inn at the
    Boathouse

Cleveland
Baricelli Inn
John Q's Steakhouse
Restaurante Giovanni's
The River View Room

Columbus
Bravo! Cucina

Youngstown
Boat Yard Ltd.
Mr. P's Café & Bakery

OKLAHOMA

Choctaw
Old Germany Restaurant

OREGON

Bend
Riverhouse

Portland
Jake's Famous Crawfish
McCormick & Schmick's
    Seafood
Sports Den • Shilo Inn

PENNSYLVANIA

Philadelphia
Chester Valley Golf Club
Chris' Café
London Grill
Palm Restaurant
Philip's Italian Restaurant
Le Bec Fin Bar
Zanzibar Blue

Pittsburgh
Jake's Above the Square
Le Mont
Fox Chapel Yacht Club
Morton's of Chicago

Bristol
King George II Inn

Lafayette
Eagle Lodge Conference
    Resort

RHODE ISLAND

Providence
Capital Grille
Turks Head Club

Newport
Cliff Walk Manor

SOUTH CAROLINA

Charleston
Country Club of Charleston
Smoking Lamp
Ship's Bounty Restaurant

SOUTH DAKOTA

Alcester
Alcester Steakhouse

Sioux Falls
Theo's Great Food

Rapid City
Window on Dakota

TENNESSEE

Memphis
Mallard's • Peabody Hotel

Nashville
Arthur's
The Merchant's Restaurant
Morton's of Chicago

TEXAS

Amarillo
Expresso To Go

Austin
Louis 106 Grill & Tapas Bar
Four Seasons Hotel
Mezzaluna

Dallas
Bob's Steak & Chop House
Del Frisco's Double Eagle
    Steakhouse
Ewalds • Stoneleigh Hotel
The French Room • The
    Adolphus Hotel
Nana Grill
Mansion On Turtle Creek

Fort Worth
Michael's

Houston
Bar & Grill • Ritz Carlton
Charley's
DeVille Café • Four Seasons
    Hotel
Monesano Ristorante Italiano
Ruggles

San Antonio
Morton's of Chicago
Pour La France

El Paso
Café Central

VERMONT

Stowe
Ye Olde England Inne

Wilmington
Hermitage Inn

West Dover
The Inn at Sawmill Farm

Norwich
La Poule a Dents

VIRGINIA

Arlington
Coco's Casa Mia Ristorante

Richmond
Du Jour
The Tobacco Co. Restaurant
The Hill Café
Assembly • Commonwealth
    Park Suites Hotel

Virginia Beach
The Lighthouse Restaurant
Traditions

Alexandria
Morrison House

McLean
Evans Farm Inn
The Sitting Duck Pub

Williamsburg
The Dining Room • Ford's
    Colony

Middleburg
Tuscany Inn

WASHINGTON

Seattle
Aoki Sushi Bar and Grill
Daniel's Broiler
F. X. McRory's Steak, Chop
    & Oyster House
McCormick's Fish House
    and Bar
Crepe de Paris
Franglor's Creole Café
Wild Ginger Asian Restaurant
    & Satay Bar

WEST VIRGINIA

Harpers Ferry
The Anvil Restaurant

White Sulphur Springs
Greenbrier Hotel

WISCONSIN

Madison
The Bistro • The Madison
  Concourse Hotel

Milwaukee
Cosmo's Top Hat Club
Racine Country Club
Joe & Mario's Ristorante
Shakers

Plymouth
Fifty Two Stafford

Wausau
Wausau Club

WYOMING

Moose
Gros Ventre River Ranch
Dornan's

Moran
Jenny Lake Lodge Lounge

INTERNATIONAL

AUSTRALIA

Melbourne
Fonteins on Lygon

Sydney
The Park Lane Sydney Hotel

AUSTRIA

Vienna
Gottfried
Restaurant Steirereck
Le Gourmet Restaurant

Karanten
Casino Restaurant Overdasso

Vorarlberg
Gasthof Torggel

BAHAMAS

Nassau
Graycliff

BELGIUM

Antwerp
Careme

Brussels
Bruneau
La Truffe Noire
Maison du Boeuf

Bermuda
Henry VIII

BRAZIL

Sao Paulo
Massimo
Roane

CANADA

BRITISH COLOMBIA

Vancouver
The Cannery Seafood
  Restaurant
Chartwheel Restaurant • Four
  Seasons Hotel

ONTARIO

Minaki
Minaki Lodge Dining Room •
  Four Seasons Hotel

Ottawa
Carleton Dining Room •
  Hilton Carleton

Toronto
Al Fresco Ristorante
Babsi's
Carlo and Adelina's
Clair de Lune
Le Petit Gourmet
Mary Johns Restaurant
Pepos Bistro
The Senator
Winston's

QUEBEC

Montreal
Bistro a Champlain
Le Biment Rouge
Le Lutetia

Quebec City
L'Inox
Restaurant Le Balico

CROATIA

Zagreb
Gracanska

DENMARK

Copenhagen
Kommandanten
Restaurant Kanalen
Restaurationen

FINLAND

Helsinki
Lord

FRANCE

Lyons
Leon de Lyon
Paul Bocuse

Marseilles
Le Petit Nice

Paris
Au Trou Gascon
Carre des Feuillants
Espadon
Gerard Besson
Jamin
L'Espadon
La Cagouille
Lucas Carton
Taillevent
Tour d'Argent

Strasbourg
Buerechiesel
Le Crocodile

GERMANY

Berlin
Casa de Espana
Rockendorf's Restaurant

Cologne
Rino Casati
Maritim Hotel

Dusseldorf
Im Schiffen
La Grappa
Restaurant Landsknecht

Frankfurt
Die Ente vom Lehel
Weinhaus Bruckenkeller

Hamburg
Le Canard
Au Mandarin Restaurant
Fischereihafen Restaurant
Landhous Scherer

Munich
Konigshof
Restaurant Aubergine

GUAM

Tamuning
Creations

GUATEMALA

Guatemala City
Jake's

HONG KONG

Brown's • The Peninsula
    Hotel
Cigar Divan • The Mandarin
    Hotel

IRELAND

Dublin
Le Coq Hardi

ITALY

Florence
Enoteca Pinchiorri

Milan
A Riccione
Gualtiero Marchesi
Scaletta

Rome
Papa Giovanni
Relais le Jardin • Hotel Lord
    Byron
Restaurant Sans Souci

Venice
Harry's Bar

JAMAICA

Kingston
The Restaurant • Temple Hall
    Estate

JAPAN

Osaka
Chez Wada

Tokyo
Apicius
Azabudai
Enoteca
Haut Brion
Keyaki Grill
Palazzo Royal Park Hotel
Prunier Tokyo Kaikan
Sabatini

Yokohama
Azur • Yokohama Grand
    Intercontinental Hotel

LUXEMBOURG

Luxembourg
Patin d'Or
St. Michel

MEXICO

Mexico City
Bellinghausen
Champs Elysees
Delmonic's
Ciculo del Sureste
Fonda del Recuerdo
La Hacienda de los Morales
Les Moustaches
Loredo
Passy
Remi

MONACO

Monte Carlo
Grill de l'Hotel de Paris
Restaurant Louis XV • Hotel
   de Paris

NETHERLANDS

Amsterdam
Christophe
Halvemaan
Le Restaurant Tout Court
Haesje Claes Restaurant

Haarlem
De Bokkedoorns
De Oude Rosmolen

NORWAY

Oslo
Bagatelle

POLAND

Krakow
Wierzynek Restaurant

PORTUGAL

Lisbon
Casa da Comida
Coventual
Tagide Largo da Academia

PUERTO RICO

San Juan
Dar Tiffany

Hato Rey
Bankers Club of Puerto Rico

Cabo Rojo
Perichi's • Hotel Parado

SOUTH KOREA

Seoul
Westin Chosun Hotel

SOUTH AFRICA

Capetown
Green Dolphin
Grill Room • Mount Nelson
   Hotel

Johannesburg
Baccarat
Bentley's
Chapters
Coachman's Inn
Falcon Crest
Horatio's
Ile de France
Le Beaujolais
Leipoldt's
Marialya
Parreirinha
Sausalito
Vilamoura
Zoo Lake Restaurant

SPAIN

Barcelona
Botafumeiro
Eldorano Petit
Jaume de Provenca
Neichel
Via Veneto

Madrid
Café de Orente
El Olivo
El Pescador
La Trainera
Luculo
Senorio de Bertiz
Zalacain

SWITZERLAND

Crissier
Fredy Girardet

Geneva
Hotel de la Cigogne
Le Chat Botte • Hotel Beau
   Rivage
Le Cygne

Zurich
Conti da Bianca
Gassthof zum Baren
Gourmet Hotel Zurich
Taverna Catalana
La Cite Rosa Tschudi
Witschi's Resaurant

THAILAND

Bangkok
Albero & Grana
Oriental Hotel

UNITED KINGDOM

London
The Berkley Restaurant
Butlers Wharf Chop House
Cantina del Ponte
Cornucopia
Claridges
Le Gauroche Restaurant
Le Pont de la Tour
Mosimann's
Overtons Restaurant
Quaglino's
Savoy Grill
Simpsons-in-the-Strand

VIRGIN ISLANDS

St. Croix
The Galleon
The Great House at
    Villa Madeleine

VENEZUELA

Caracas
Primi

SPEAKING OF CIGARS:
Words to Smoke By

The lingo, the buzz words, and the serious language that you need for cigar speak are here.

Aging • The period during which newly completed cigars rest in humidity controlled, cedar-lined storage areas, called "aging rooms." This rest time gives the flavors of the tobaccos within the cigars a chance to blend.

A.M.S. • **American Market Selection**. A designation for the light and mild wrappers, Claro Claro, Candela, and Jade.

Aroma • A cigar's smell when it is burning. **Bouquet** is the smell of the wrapper and open foot before the cigar has been lit.

Band • The paper ring around each cigar that decoratively identifies the brand.

Barrel • The shaft of the cigar. Also called the **body** or canon (pronounced *canyon*).

Biddies • A small East Indian cigar.

Binder • The tobacco leaf wrapped around the filler, holding the core of the cigar together. The outer or wrapper leaf covers the binder.

Blend The combination of tobacco leaves chosen for each cigar. A cigar's character depends on the blend, which may have tobaccos from different countries, crops, and years. The blender strives for a mixture that results in a consistent good taste.

Booking • Folding the filler leaves in a cigar's bunch the way the pages of a book are folded. This is an inferior method, causing a thicker concentration of leaves on one side, which results in uneven taste and burning.

Buckeye • A small, generally family owned, cigar-making company.

Bulks • The tall stacks of tobacco piled high so that fermentation will take place as the temperature within them rises. Also called *burros*, a Cuban term.

Bunch • During cigar making, the leaves that make up the filler and binder before the finishing wrapper leaf is added.

Bunchbreaker • The person in a cigar factory who takes the filler and wraps a binder leaf around it, creating a bunch. Also called a *buncher* or *bunchmaker*.

Cap • The piece of tobacco laid over the head of a cigar. It is clipped before smoking.

Casing • A process of spraying tobacco after it has been dried. This remoisturizing makes the leaves pliable so that they can be rolled into cigars.

Clear Havana • An all-Havana cigar.

Criollos • Harsh cigars smoked by native Cubans.

Culebra • A three-in-one twisted cigar. Actually three corkscrew-shaped cigars bound together. An invention of cigar factories of the nineteenth century to keep workers from stealing their product. Each employee was allowed three cigars a day—of this obvious shape only.

Curly Head • The little ponytail-like twisted end of tobacco on the head of some premium-brand cigars. Also called *fancy tail*.

Demitasse • A small sized cigar, usually 4 inches long with a 30 ring gauge.

Dry Cigars • Called dry or "Dutch type" by Americans, these small cigars need no humidification. Made by the Dutch and Swiss, they use short filler, usually of tobacco from Sumatra and Indonesia, but also Cuban.

E.M.S. • **English Market Selection.** A term for the rich brown wrapper color favored in Great Britain and America.

Fermentation • The process during which cigar tobacco,

through self-generated heat, gives off nicotine and other compounds, turns color, and gains much of its flavor. Also called "curing," "sweating," or "mulling."

Figuardo • A cigar that is not a straight-sided cylinder such as a Pyramid or Torpedo.

Filler • The blend of tobacco in the center of the cigar surrounded by the binder and then the wrapper. The heart of a cigar's flavor.

Finished Head • The head of a cigar that has been formed by the wrapper leaf, not a separate cap.

Flathead • A cigar whose head is not rounded, but flat.

Foot • The end of the cigar that is lit. Also called the "tuck" end.

Galera • The large factory room where the cigars are rolled.

Guillotine • A cigar cutter that works like its namesake: the hand-held instrument has a hole where the head of the cigar is placed, and a blade to slice off a circular opening. A "guillotine cut" describes the cut.

Hand • A group of about twenty tobacco leaves that are tied together at the bottom of their stems. In processing and sorting, the hand is the division generally used.

Handmade • A cigar that has been bunched and rolled completely by hand.

Handrolled • A cigar whose wrapper has been added by hand, but whose bunch was made by machine. Sometimes designated (erroneously) as handmade.

Head • The end of the cigar that is clipped and put into the mouth.

Homogenized Tobacco Leaf (HTL) • A tobacco product that is used for binder and sometimes wrapper in some "dry" European cigars and American mass-market cigars. It is made from tobacco scraps combined with substances like cellulose and pressed to form sheets.

Humidor • An airtight box, usually of wood, with a humidifying element for storing cigars.

Hygrometer • An instrument that measures relative humidity. In regard to cigars, it can be used in a humidor.

Long Filler • The filler in premium cigars, long enough to fill the entire length of the body.

Marble Head • A round-headed cigar.

Marrying • Different tobaccos in a cigar are said to "marry" when their oils and aromas permeate one another, creating a blend. The "aging room" in a cigar factory is also called the "marrying room."

Mass-Market Cigar • A reference to all low-priced cigars manufactured by machine in large quantities.

Naked • Term used to describe a cigar not covered by cellophane or a tube.

Notch Cutter • A cigar cutter that creates a V-shaped opening in the head.

Plug • An obstruction in the cigar, caused by tightness in the rolling, that makes drawing difficult.

Plume • A white or light grayish-green dusting on a cigar's wrapper, caused by the crystallization of tobacco oils. Not mold, it is harmless and can be brushed off. Also called "bloom," it occurs most often in cigars kept in a humidor quite some time.

Premium Cigar • Any high grade cigar made by hand of one-hundred percent tobacco with long leaf filler.

Puro • Spanish for pure, the term refers to a cigar whose filler, binder, and wrapper are made from tobacco grown in the same country.

Ring Gauge • A measurement for the diameter of a cigar divided into sixty-fourths. Thus a 64 ring gauge would mean that a cigar had a one-inch diameter. A 32 ring gauge indicates a half-inch diameter; a 48, a three-quarters inch diameter.

Roller ● The person who applies the wrapper leaf to the bunch in cigar making. Master rollers are highly skilled craftsmen.

Scrap Filler ● Leftover tobacco cuttings used as filler for inexpensive cigars.

Shade Leaf ● Tobacco grown under a canopy of cheese-cloth or mesh to shield it from the sun. Most often used in reference to Connecticut shade leaf wrapper.

Short Filler ● Not the same as scrap filler, short filler is made of premium tobacco long filler leaves cut to a smaller size so they can be used in small cigars or in manufacturing by machines.

Smoker ● Broadly defined, a cigar smoking event. This can be an elaborate meal with wines and cigars for each course, or a more informal gathering of like-minded cigar aficionados.

Stogie or Stogy ● Slang for cigar, often inexpensive. Invented in 1827 and smoked by frontiersmen heading west, the cigar was said to resemble the spoke of a Conestoga wagon wheel. First the cigar was called Conestoga, and then it was shortened to the stubby name stogy.

Tooth ● Tiny, gritty bumps that are part of the natural texture of some tobacco wrapper leaves.

Torcedor ● The Cuban term for master cigar roller.

Tuck ● Also called the "foot" of the cigar, the end that is lit.

Wrapper ● The outer leaf rolled around the binder. Wrapper is the finest-quality leaf on any cigar.